German Operation at Anzio: A Study of the German Operations at Anzio Beachhead from: 22 Jan 44 to 31 May 44, Part 2

Military Intelligence Division, War Department

The BiblioGov Project is an effort to expand awareness of the public documents and records of the U.S. Government via print publications. In broadening the public understanding of government and its work, an enlightened democracy can grow and prosper. Ranging from historic Congressional Bills to the most recent Budget of the United States Government, the BiblioGov Project spans a wealth of government information. These works are now made available through an environmentally friendly, print-on-demand basis, using only what is necessary to meet the required demands of an interested public. We invite you to learn of the records of the U.S. Government, heightening the knowledge and debate that can lead from such publications.

Included are the following Collections:

Budget of The United States Government
Presidential Documents
United States Code
Education Reports from ERIC
GAO Reports
History of Bills
House Rules and Manual
Public and Private Laws

Code of Federal Regulations
Congressional Documents
Economic Indicators
Federal Register
Government Manuals
House Journal
Privacy act Issuances
Statutes at Large

of the woods at Bosco di Padiglione (F 880260). Local counterattacks may be expected, especially against the flanks of our assault groups. Heavy enemy losses are no indication that enemy resistance will diminish.

C. Statistics

German losses: (less 29th Panzer Grenadier Division, 114th Jäger Division and 715th Infantry Division): 63 killed, 350 wounded, and 21 missing.

Allied losses: 364 prisoners (293 Americans mostly from 179th Infantry Regiment and 2d Battalion 180th Infantry Regiment.) 14 tanks (4 Sherman) destroyed, 1 antitank gun destroyed, 4 airplanes downed by antiaircraft guns, and 2 ammunition carriers and 4 personnel carriers set afire. Captured: 4 Sherman tanks, 2 antiaircraft guns (2 cm), 17 machine guns, 1 mortar, 1 bazooka with rockets, 30 rifles, 12 automatic pistols, and 1 antitank rifle.

XXVI. 19 FEBRUARY 1944

A. Operations Report

During the day, strong enemy counterattacks, supported by tanks, forced partial withdrawals from newly gained positions.

Heavy enemy artillery fire resulted in great losses and halted the attack of the 65th Infantry Division at Cle Buon Riposo (F 859310). However, the 65th Infantry Division's left flank advanced towards the south, and in a simultaneous attack from the east by parts of the LXXVI Panzer Corps, the strongpoint Cle Buon Riposo was encircled.

During heavy night fighting, the bridgehead south of the forest Macchia della Ficoccia, 2 km southeast Aprilia (F 875333), was enlarged. But in the afternoon, enemy counterattacks launched with tank support, forced back the 114th Jäger Division into the northern part of the forest. The division suffered considerable losses in men and materiel. The village of Cle l'Ovile, 1 km east Cantoniera (F 864282), was captured by combat patrols of the 26th Panzer and 29th Panzer Grenadier Divisions. It was lost again, during an enemy tank attack, in the evening. Assault troops of the 29th Panzer Grenadier Division crossed highway 82 (F 780300 - F 922290), in a front 500 meters wide. The right flank of Panzer Division "Hermann Göring", attacking Colle del Pozzo, 2 km west Cle Carano (F 940309), was stopped in front of the enemy positions by concentrated defensive fire. The left flank occupied two hills northeast of Colle del Pozzo.

The 1028th Panzer Grenadier Regiment is attached to the 715th Infantry Division. This Division was stationed in the region southeast of Aprilia as Corps Reserve. It now will take over the left sector of the LXXVI Panzer Corps, adjacent to the 114th Jäger Division as of 0800, 20 February 1944.

The enemy continued to place concentrated fire on the main line of resistance and interrupted supply lines by heavy harrassing fire. During our attack, Allied artillery fired barrages irrespective of their own main line of resistance. The increased fire of enemy artillery and the continuous air raids by bombers and fighter bombers leads to the conclusion that the enemy intends to hold the positions on Highway 82. During the morning, Fourteenth Army informed Army Group by phone that a shift of the main effort to the east would require vast preparations, and would be advantageous to the enemy.

Therefore, we intend to destroy enemy forces isolated in the region of Cle Buon Riposo (F 859310), by a converging attack from all sides, and to consolidate the situation on the eastern flank of the LXXVI Panzer Corps (114th Jäger Division). All forces available will attack along highway Cle Carroceto (F 869330) - Torre di Padiglione (F 921289). Occupation of Highway 82 by surprise attacks will be attempted in the sectors of the LXXVI Panzer Corps, 3rd Panzer Grenadier Division, and 26th Panzer Division. After clearing the situation on both flanks of the attack group, Army intends to initiate, as soon as possible, a decisive southwesterly attack, in the sector of the 29th Panzer Grenadier Division.

The 26th Panzer Division will be made available for employment in the new offensive sector in the direction Torre di Padiglione, as soon as the situation on the western flank has been cleared up. The 362nd Division has been transferred from the coast defense sector Cecina - mouth of the Tiber to replace the Panzer Division "Hermann Göring" will be used for attacks in the sector of the LXXVI Panzer Corps. The former sector of the 362nd Infantry Division will be taken over by the newly activated 92nd Infantry Division, whose present strength is 4,242 men. The 954th Grenadier Regiment of the 362nd Infantry Division (Army Group C Reserve) will be transferred from the area of Pescara to an area south of Rome. The 2nd Battalion 1027th Panzer Grenadier Regiment and the Regimental Staff, until now employed in the coast defense sector Cecina - mouth of the Tiber, have been attached to the 65th Infantry Division.

The 146th Grenadier Regiment of the 65th Infantry Division, at present attached to the Tenth Army, will return to its division by 15 March. The combat strength of the 65th Infantry Division is 26 officers, and 871 enlisted men.

B. Intelligence Report

The following new units have been identified: 3rd Battalion 180th Infantry Regiment is located in the area east and north-east of Maccia della Ficoccia; the 514th Company Royal Army Service Corps of the 56th Infantry Division (Br) is near the highway in the region of Campo di Carne (F 870285).

The enemy artillery fired 30,000 rounds on 19 February 1944.

Our attacks have confused the enemy and also brought about emergency situations in some of his units. The enemy command has repeatedly called upon isolated and dangerously placed units to hold their positions, by promising reinforcements. Having determined the main direction of our attack, the enemy probably will concentrate all available forces in the region south of Aprilia to intercept the attack at the wood of Padiglione (F 890260). As the territory north of the forest has been lost, the enemy lacks observation posts. In addition, the loss of the northern edges of the forest has endangered his artillery positions. Stubborn opposition from key positions at the cross roads at Campo di Carne (F 863285), and Fta Padiglione (F 857242), and the traffic centers Torre di Padiglione (F 922289) and Le Ferriere (F 933342), is expected. Increased counterattacks, supported by tanks, against our flanks and especially southwest of Spaccasassi (F 917330) are imminent. It is estimated that large parts of the enemy's infantry and tank reserves were committed in today's counterattack, viz. the 1st Infantry Division (Br) and 1st Armored Division (US).

C. Statistics

German losses: (loss 4th Parachute Division, 3rd Panzer
Grenadier Division, and 114th Jäger Division) 48 killed, 167
wounded, and 25 missing.

Allied losses: 83 prisoners, and 10 tanks destroyed.

XXVII. 20 FEBRUARY 1944

A. Operations Report

As a result of our attack from the west, the enemy was completely
surrounded at Cle Buon Riposo (F 859310), and a defensive front toward
the south was established. During the day, an enemy tank attack was
repelled.

The 3rd Panzer Grenadier Division seized the eastern edge of
the Gorge Campo di Carne (F 850890 to F 270290), the southwest edge
of the Gorge Fosso di Carente, 700 meters northwest of Cantoniera
(F 862282), and moved up to a line, 600 meters north of the crossroads of Cantoniera. The battalions of the 29th Panzer Grenadier
Division (3rd and 1st Battalions 15th Grenadier Regiment), which had
crossed Highway 82, east of Fta. Campo di Carne the day before, were
either wiped out or were dispersed. The 114th Jäger Division in
another attack from the northwest, seized the southern edge of the
Macchia della Ficoccia forest, 3 km southeast of Aprilic (F 875333).
An enemy tank attack towards Cle Rosatelli (F 908320) was repulsed.

We aim to destroy the enemy troops surrounded in the area of
Buon Riposo (F 859310), and to prevent a breakthrough from the southwest, designed to assist these encircled troops. To avoid losses,
Fourteenth Army ordered that the Panther tanks, brought up to clear
the pocket of Buon Riposo, be used only as armored artillery.

In order to straighten the main line of resistance, on the
eastern flank of the LXVI Panzer Corps, an attack will be launched,
as early as possible on 21 February, to seize the enemy strongpoints
Cle Biadaretto 2 km north of Cle Torre di Padiglione (F 921289) and
Cle Carano (F 940309).

During our attempt to clear the pocket at Cle Buon Riposo
(F 859310), the enemy bombarded his own positions with heavy artillery fire. His troops were protected against this, as they had taken
shelter in the caves of the ravines to be found in that terrain. Our
own fire could not reach them. Our units lost many radio sets, due
to the heavy enemy artillery shells, the concussion of which destroyed
the tubes.

It has become very difficult to evacuate the wounded. All
ambulances, including the armored ones have been lost, making it
necessary to use assault guns and Tiger tanks for the evacuation.

By early morning of 23 February, 2 Battalions of the 15th
Panzer Grenadier Division, previously employed on the Cassino
front, will be attached to the 29th Panzer Grenadier Division. The
remaining elements of the 735th Grenadier Regiment 715th Infantry
Division, i.e., 2 officers, 25 noncommissioned officers, and 158
men were assigned to the combat team of the 725th Grenadier Regiment.

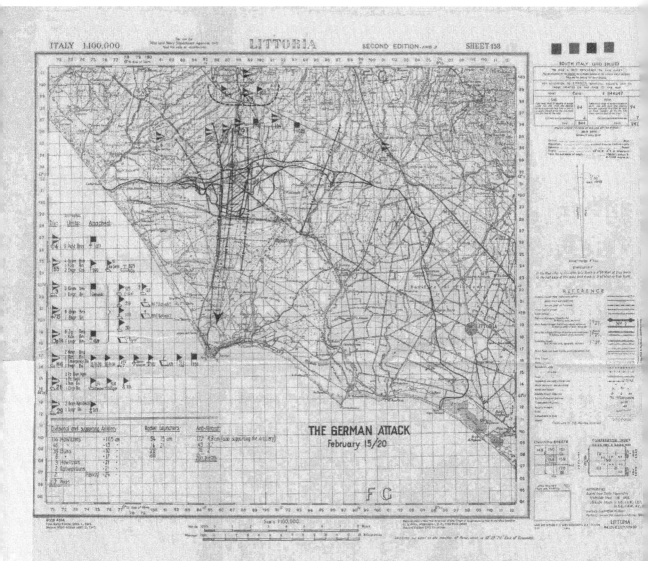

The German Attack, February 15/20 — LITTORIA, Sheet 158, Italy 1:100,000 (Second Edition)

B. Intelligence Report

According to reliable sources, the 6th Armored Infantry Regiment 1st Armored Division (US), with attached tanks, is in the sector of the 157th Infantry Regiment. One of the battalions of the 6th Regiment is employed west of the Aprilia-Nettuno Highway and two battalions east of it. The Commanding Officer of the 1st King's Shropshire Light Infantry is Lt. Col. Carelass, and the Commanding Officer of S Company 1st King's Shropshire Light Infantry is Major Mausabb. Major Brook commands Company C 1st London Irish Rifles.

On 19 February, the enemy supplied his surrounded troops, at Cle Buon Riposo, by air. Air reconnaissance reports show active disembarkation in the Anzio-Nettuno harbor.

C. Statistics

German losses (less 114th Jäger Division and 15th Motorized Grenadier Regiment): 61 dead, 211 wounded, and 8 missing.

Total losses from 16 to 20 February 1944 (dead, wounded, and missing): 5,389 men.

Allied losses: 62 prisoners (53 British, 9 Americans) and 1 tank put out of commission.

According to prisoner of war reports, the enemy lost many heavy infantry weapons.

XXVIII. 21 FEBRUARY 1944

A. Operations Report

In the evening of 20 February, preceded by heavy artillery fire, the enemy repeatedly attacked along the entire sector of the 29th Panzer Grenadier Division, and pushed back the left flank to a position some 2 km northwest of Torre di Padiglione (F 921289). There, a German counterattack, during the early morning hours, regained the formerly held positions at the Fosso delle Vallicelette, 3 km west of Torre di Padiglione.

At 0430, the 715th Infantry Division attacked to seize Cle Biadaretto, 2 km north of Torre di Padiglione, and Cle Carano (F940309). Heavy defense fire from the enemy stopped the attack. At 1730, after the enemy lines had been subjected to artillery fire and fighter bomber attack, another attack was attempted, but due to strong enemy defenses, the objective could not be reached. Enemy assaults in company strength, supported by tanks, were repulsed by the 114th Jäger Division.

Concentrated artillery fire destroyed enemy infantry and tank positions. Long-range artillery shelled the Anzio harbor, disembarkation points southeast of Nettuno, and supply depots. Antiaircraft artillery played an important role in the destruction of supply routes.

The enemy fighter bombers were less active than during the previous days. The Panzer Division "Hermann Göring", which is to

be employed in the Spaccasassi sector (F 917330) for offensive
operations, was relieved, at 1200, by the 362d Infantry Division.
The Combat Team "von Corvin" consisting of: 1st Battalion 2d
Panzer Grenadier Regiment "Hermann Göring", 2d Battalion 1st
Panzer Grenadier Regiment "Hermann Göring", and Panzer Recon-
naissance Battalion "Hermann Göring" was attached to the 715th
Infantry Division.

Our aims are: First, the destruction of enemy positions at
Cle Buon Riposo (F 859310) by the morning of 22 February. Second,
the immediate relief of the forces of the 3d Panzer Grenadier
Division west of the Aprilia-Nettuno highway, by the I Parachute
Corps. Before the morning of 25 February, the 3d Panzer Grenadier
Division will relieve the 26th Panzer Division and parts of the
western flank of the 29th Panzer Grenadier Division. The 26th
Panzer Division will be shifted to the area north of Cle Tre
Spaccasassi (F 917330), before dawn of 26 February. Third, the
seizure of the Colle del Pozzo, 2 km west of Cle Carano (F 940309),
by the western flank of the 362d Infantry Division about 24 February.

B. Intelligence Report

The 1st Battalion 504th Parachute Regiment (US) is employed
in the sector Fosso Formal del Bove, west of Colle del Pozzo.
American infantry is on the right flank; on the left are additional
paratroopers.

Increased naval activity was observed in the harbor of Anzio-
Nettuno. Aerial reconnaissance reports indicate the presence of
6 merchant ships approximate tonnage: 10,000 to 15,000 tons each,
2 medium transports, one cruiser, and 7 destroyers.

C. Statistics

German losses: 85 killed, 236 wounded, and 8 missing.

Allied losses: 4 tanks destroyed, 1 tank rendered immobile,
1 radio station captured.

XXIX. 22 FEBRUARY 1944

A. Operations Report

The attack to destroy the enemy pocket at Cle Buon Riposo
(F 859310), did not succeed. Under a heavy enemy barrage, the
troops had to fight in difficult terrain with deep ravines. Up
to the present, 150 prisoners have been brought in.

In the morning, and again in the afternoon, the 715th Infantry
Division attacked Cle Biadaretto, 2 km north of Cle di Padiglione
(F 921289), and the Cle Carano hills (F 940309). However, due to
the enemy's defensive fire, these attacks were halted short of
their objectives.

At 1900, the 3d Panzer Grenadier Division took over the
sector formerly occupied by the 26th Panzer Division. The 67th
Panzer Grenadier Regiment of the 26th Panzer Division, was attached
to the 3d Panzer Grenadier Division.

To complete its mission successfully, the Fourteenth Army requested the Commander in Chief Southwest to strengthen it with one complete division ready for combat service, possibly a mountain division for greater mobility in wooded areas; one heavy mortar and one medium howitzer battalion; one engineer assault battalion; and additional portable radio sets, of which the Army has a shortage of 468.

We intend to shorten the main line of resistance on the east flank of the LXXVI Panzer Corps by seizing the Biadaretto and Carano hills, as well as to destroy, as quickly as possible, all enemy units still in the area Cle Buon Riposo (F 859310), in order to relieve units of the 3d Panzer Grenadier Division in the area west of the highway.

After the 3d Panzer Grenadier Division has taken over the present sector of the 26th Panzer Division and parts of the western flank of the 29th Panzer Grenadier Division, it will be attached to the I Parachute Corps. When fighting has ceased, in the area of Ble Biadaretto, the remaining units of the 715th Infantry Division will be withdrawn in order to take over the sector of two battalions on the eastern flank of the 362d Infantry Division. All forces committed south of that area will be attached to the 715th Division.

On or about 26 February the Army plans a breakthrough to the Mussolini Canal, from the north, crossing a general line from Pte della Crocetta (F 950296) to Isola Bella (G 006294). Units to participate in this attack will be: 362d Infantry Division, Panzer Division "Hermann Göring", and the 26th Panzer Division. The attack will be made from the west flank of the 362d Infantry Division. If this action meets with success, the Army intends to push on to the lower Spaccasassi creek (F 9229 to F 992253). The two battalions of the 15th Panzer Grenadier Division (earmarked for the 29th Panzer Grenadier Division) which are at present in transit will be held initially as Army reserve in the area west of Velletri. After the 29th Panzer Grenadier Division has been withdrawn from its present front sector, it will be used either for the attack against Fosso di Spaccasassi and to roll up the enemy lines southwest of Cisterna (G 0232) from the west; or to make a surprise attack from north of the area of Borgo Podgora (G 045240) against the enemy units fighting in the area of Isola Bella.

Experience has shown that the enemy reacts very quickly to a regrouping of our forces. It is, therefore, imperative that the regrouping be concealed, and it is of particular importance that the enemy be engaged along the entire line by continuous raids. These raids will have the secondary purpose of improving the local front. By means of all types of deceptive measures, the enemy must be misled as to the actual assembly area of the assault divisions. To aid this deception further, the I Parachute Corps will erect dummy tanks in the area around Ardea (F 787350).

By order of Hitler, tank assaults in small groups will be made prior to the attack from and south of the area of Borgo Podgora in the direction of the Mussolini Canal. The tanks of the Panzer Division "Hermann Göring", used for this purpose, will return to their division shortly before the attack begins.

The objective of this attack is to push back the beachhead in the sector of the LXXVI Panzer Corps toward the general line from Fosso di Leschione (F 885300 to F 917289) to Fosso di Spaccasassi up to the point where it joins the Mussolini Canal, 1.5 km west of Borgo Podgora.

B. **Intelligence Report**

2d Company, 7th Queens (169th Brigade, 56th Infantry Division) (Br) located in Fosso della Bottaccia, 1 km northwest of Fta Campo di Carne (F 862284) has been identified by 16 prisoners of war. Presence of the entire Brigade is confirmed by captured documents. 1st Battalion Irish Guards 24th Brigade, is located 150 meters southeast of Puntoni, 1 km northwest of Cantoniera (F 863282). During the night of 21 to 22 February, the 1st Irish Guards came from south of Campo di Carne to this new area, and relieved an unidentified American unit. Three days before, the 3d Company received 30 replacements from supply troops of the Battalion; the 1st Company, reduced to 38 men, was absorbed by the 3d Company. The 1st Scots Guards and the 5th Grenadier Guards 24th Brigade were committed in the night of 21 to 22 February according to prisoners of war.

Reliable sources report the enemy expects an impending attack near Campo di Carne and to the east.

C. **Statistics**

German losses: 86 killed, 232 wounded, and 84 missing.

Allied losses: 265 prisoners (75 from Cle Buon Riposo), 5 tanks destroyed, 1 self propelled antitank gun destroyed (75 mm), and 2 tanks put out of commission. Captured material: 1 antitank gun (50 mm), 11 machine guns, 1 mortar, 1 antitank rifle, and 1 bazooka.

XXX. 23 FEBRUARY 1944

A. **Operations Report**

After brief artillery preparatory fire, the 65th Infantry Division renewed its attack at 0530, against the encircled enemy at Cle Buon Riposo (F 853310). Supported by self-propelled guns, we succeeded in penetrating the enemy's defensive system, and occupied the houses at Cle Buon Riposo. With the exception of enemy remnants we cleared out the valley. Two enemy relief attacks, in battalion strength from the south, were repulsed after heavy fighting. Our artillery shelled infantry and artillery targets, and supported the attack on Cle Buon Riposo with blocking fire towards the south.

During the night of 22 to 23 February, the 725th Grenadier Regiment 715th Infantry Division, was relieved by the 2d Battalion 1028th Panzer Grenadier Regiment, and transferred to Fosso Fresciano, 4 km northeast of Campoleone (F 860406) as reserve. Combat Team "von Corvin", which had been attached to the 715th Infantry Division on 21 February, was now placed under the command of the 114th Jäger Division. At 1200, the 362d Infantry Division was attached to the LXXVI Panzer Corps.

B. **Intelligence Report**

According to prisoners, the 509th Parachute Battalion (US) is now located 1.5 km north of the Collo del Pozzo (2 km west of

Cle Carano F 940309). The Battalion is attached to the 3d Infantry Division (US). On its right is the 7th Infantry Regiment 3d Infantry Division; on its left, the 180th Infantry Regiment of the 45th Infantry Division (US).

According to interrogation of prisoners of war and captured documents, the 167th Infantry Brigade and the 169th Infantry Brigade landed on 11 and 19 February respectively.

For the past week, the boundary between the English and American sectors ran along the Aprilia-Anzio Highway. Reliable sources report that the Royal Scot Greys Armored Battalion is in the area east of the highway.

Counterattacks from the area southwest of Aprilia (F 875333), strongly supported by armor, are to be expected. Reliable sources report that part of the enemy armored forces are assembled in this area.

C. Statistics

German losses (less 3d Panzer Grenadier Division, 9th and 1027th Panzer Grenadier Regiments): 33 killed, 184 wounded, and 8 missing.

Allied losses: 402 prisoners (majority from 2d Battalion 157th Infantry Regiment, and 2d Company 7th Queen's Own), and 1 tank put out of commission.

XXXI. 24 FEBRUARY 1944

A. Operations Report

Reconnaissance and combat patrols were conducted by both sides during the period. In the sector of the I Parachute Corps, an enemy attack in company strength and a tank assault were repelled. The pocket of Cle Buon Riposo (F 859310) was cleared, with the exception of a few dispersed Allied troops. At 2030, the 10th and 11th Parachute Jäger Regiments began an attack to straighten the main line of resistance at the boundary of the 4th Parachute Division and the 65th Infantry Division.

The 3d Panzer Grenadier Division will be attached to the I Parachute Corps at noon on 25 February 1944; the Infantry Demonstration Regiment, 998th Heavy Artillery Battalion, 10th Company Artillery Demonstration Regiment, and one Company of the 525th Heavy Antitank Battalion (Hornets) are attached to this division. The new boundary line of the I Parachute Corps and the LXXVI Panzer Corps is: Stazione di Campoleone (F 877385) – Aprilia (F 875333) – Cle l'Ovile, 1 km east of Cantoniera (F 862282). Tenth Army will supply the 3d Panzer Grenadier Division with ten armored personnel carriers for the evacuation of the wounded.

One company of the 653d Antitank Battalion (Ferdinand tanks) will be attached to the LXXVI Panzer Corps. The 3d Battalion of the 1st Parachute Regiment previously committed in the sector of the Panzer Division "Hermann Göring", will return to the 1st Parachute Division (Tenth Army). The Parachute Demonstration

Battalion, up to now with the Panzer Division "Hermann Göring" will be attached to the 4th Parachute Division.

B. Intelligence Report

According to prisoner of war statements the 6th Cheshire of the 56th Infantry Division (Br) landed on 16 February. It consists of four companies and one Headquarters Company. Each company is equipped with 12 heavy machine guns. Lt Col Birch is the Commanding Officer of the battalion.

Heavy traffic on Highway 82 (F 780300 to F 922289) indicates further regroupings. It is probable, that elements of the 1st Infantry Division (Br), which are being kept in reserve, will be committed to relieve the weaker sectors of the 45th Infantry Division (US).

C. Statistics

German losses (less 3d Panzer Grenadier Division and 715th Infantry Division): 91 killed, 343 wounded, and 55 missing.

Losses of Fourteenth Army from 16 to 22 February 1944 (including materiel turned in for repair): 450 submachine guns, 430 light machine guns, 93 heavy machine guns, 6 light mortars, 56 medium mortars, 1 heavy mortar, 2 light infantry guns, 12 light antitank guns (1 salvagable), 1 medium antitank gun, 8 heavy antitank guns, 13 light field howitzers (12 salvagable), 7 heavy field howitzers (7 salvagable), 3 guns 10 cm (3 salvagable), 1 light gun, 6 guns 7.5 cm, 1 howitzer 22 cm, 5 antiaircraft guns 2 cm (2 salvagable), 5 rocket launchers 15 cm, and 10 rocket launchers 21 cm.

Allied losses: 59 prisoners (this makes a total of 650 prisoners, taken in the pocket of Cle Buon Riposo) and 2 tanks put out of commission.

A. Operations Report.

During the night, the 4th Parachute Division and 65th Infantry Division succeeded in pushing the main line of resistance forward, despite heavy enemy artillery and mortar fire. This attack was part of the operation to straighten the line.

Late in the evening, the enemy attacked the sector of the 65th Infantry Division at the Michele Gorge (F 828315 to F 845308), and 1 km northwest of Cantoniera (F 863282). At both points the attack was made under support of heavy artillery fire, but was stopped by the coordinated fire of our artillery. No major operations, except raids, took place in the sector of the LXXVI Panzer Corps.

The following is an order for a new attack against the beach-head:

On 28 February, the Army will resume its attack against the beachhead. The LXXVI Panzer Corps will attack at 0400; in the sector of the 362d Infantry Division the attack will begin at 0545. The objective is to drive the enemy into the sea. To achieve surprise, deception and secrecy are paramount.

The I Parachute Corps is to feign preparations for an impending large-scale attack in its sector, as well as to increase activity by assault detachments, during the night of 27 to 28 February. Roving guns are to be employed in the area of Ardea (F 787350) to simulate the concentration of a new artillery group. The arrival of strong, motorized forces in the area of Ardea is to be simulated during the 26th, 27th, and in the night of 27 to 28 February. For this purpose combat vehicles of the 3d Panzer Grenadier Division will be used. Individual vehicles will be ordered to blink their lights while moving up, during the night, but this must not be done in a clumsy way. In the evening of 27 February, an attack to seize Hills 78 and 79, 1 km north of Fta. Campo di Carne (F 862284), is to be executed.

At 0530 on 28 February, our artillery will shell known enemy assembly areas, in which there will probably be heavy troop concentrations.

The LXXVI Panzer Corps is to simulate an impending strong attack in the direction of the Mussolini Canal, by tank supported raids and the use of roving guns. These operations will not be extended farther than Borgo Piave (G 053203).

In the sector where the actual attack is planned, raiding and scouting will be carried out in usual strength only. No units, other than those at present employed in these sectors, will be used in these operations. Scouting or raiding by mobile units is prohibited. During the attack, it will be important that bridge-heads are established on the south bank of the Astura creek. These brigeheads will serve as bases for further attacks.

The enemy forces remaining on both flanks of our Assault Group must be wiped out in a frontal attack by the reserves of the Army Group.

The Air Force is requested to provide air-ground support for our attacking forces, and to chase off enemy artillery observation planes, especially on 28 February.

The 65th Infantry Division reported that as a result of recent actions the conditions of its infantry is such that only an immediate relief can prevent complete exhaustion. The combat strength on 23 February was: 33 officers, 81 noncommissioned officers, and 559 enlisted men. This number includes two regimental staffs, and some regimental units. Nearly all competent noncommissioned officers and specialists were lost during recent actions. The Division will receive 400 to 800 men as replacements (surplus personnel of the 362d Infantry Division). Fourteenth Army suggests that according to development of the situation, single battalions be withdrawn for ten to fourteen days, as the current situation does not warrant the withdrawal of entire divisions.

At 1200 hours, the 715th Infantry Division took over the sector of the 362d Infantry Division which was withdrawn for the coming offensive. The divisions designated for the attack on 28 February are already in their respective assembly areas. The 1st and 2d Battalion of the 115th Panzer Grenadier Regiment arrived in the area of Cori (G 095380). These two battalions were part of the 15th Panzer Grenadier Division (Tenth Army), and are now attached to the Fourteenth Army as reserve.

B.   Intelligence Report

During the last days, the enemy attempted to regroup his disorganized units. It was established that American units were relieved by the 56th and 1st Infantry Division (Br), which now hold the line extending from the coast to the eastern side of the Aprilia-Anzio Highway. Adjoining is the 45th Infantry Division (US), with a front line extending to the area of Cle Carno (F 940309). On the latter's right flank is the 3d Infantry Division (US). Regrouping and moving up of replacements continued. The main defensive centers are still on both sides of Fta. Campo di Carne (F 862284).

C.   Statistics

German losses: (less 65th Infantry Division) 18 killed, 51 wounded, and 9 missing.

Allied losses: 46 prisoners.

XXXIII.   26 FEBRUARY 1944

A.   Operations Report

Last night, an enemy attack in company strength supported by artillery and mortar fire, succeeded temporarily in penetrating the main line of resistance, in the sector of the 4th Parachute Division. Our immediate counterattack reestablished the main line of resistance and relieved one platoon of the 10th Parachute Regiment, which had been encircled. Except for reciprocal combat patrols, the other sectors were quiet.

At 1200, the 735th Grenadier Regiment of the 715th Motorized Infantry Division took over the sector of Group "Heidebreck", of the Panzer Regiment of the Panzer Division "Hermann Göring".

The Fourteenth Army High Command ordered that in the coming

attack, in addition to previous plans, a tank group is to push forward on the highway Spaccasassi (F 917330) – Ponte della Crocetta (F 950297). In this operation it is imperative that Carano (F 940309) be seized, during the first night, by a surprise raid. The main line of resistance at the southern flank of the LXXVI Panzer Corps is to be pushed forward, during the night 26 to 27 February, at least as far as the present line of our combat outposts. From this line, assault-detachments, supported by assault guns or tanks, will thrust forward toward the Mussolini Canal. These assaults are to be made on as broad a front as possible. The line of combat outposts will be advanced to the Mussolini Canal, or at least as close as p possible to the canal.

B. Intelligence Report

The 1st Battalion 157th Infantry Regiment of the 45th Infantry Division (U S) was confirmed to be in the area of the Lwschione bridge, 1 km west of Cle Tre di Padiglione (F 921289).

C. Statistics

German losses: 53 killed, 156 wounded, and 32 missing.

Allied losses: 19 prisoners.

XXXIV. 27 FEBRUARY 1944

A. Operations Report

No activity took place on either side, except reconnaissance and assault detachment operations. The enemy carried out reconnaissance and combat patrols against the sector held by the 715th Infantry Division. Fourteen enemy artillery batteries were located by reconnaissance. Most of them are in the western sector.

The date for the intended attack is changed from 28 to 29 February. The plans remain unchanged. Beginning the night of 27 to 28 February, the 29th Panzer Grenadier Division will be withdrawn from the front, and concentrated in the area Lanuvio-Genzano-Palomba. These movements are to be completed before dawn 1 March. The 146th Grenadier Regiment, which is arriving from the Cassino area, will take over the sector of the 29th Panzer Grenadier Division. Elements of the 129th Reconnaissance Battalion (motorized), one light artillery battalion, and elements of the 525th Antitank Battalion ("Hornets") will remain in this sector.

B. Intelligence Report

Company A 2d Battalion 5th Queens (169th Brigade/56th British Infantry Division) is in the area of Michele Gorge (F 828315 to F 845308), according to prisoner of war interrogations.

C. Statistics

German losses: 44 killed, 177 wounded, 15 missing.

Allied losses: 39 prisoners, 1 tank destroyed by a mine, and several machine guns and small arms were captured.

A. Operations Report

Following up the attack by the 65th Infantry Division on 25 February, the left flank of the 4th Parachute Division pushed forward at the eastern end of the Michele Gorge (F 828315 to F 845308). In a sudden raid in the morning, the 65th Infantry Division took the group of ruined houses 1 km southwest Cle Buon Riposo (F 859310). Simultaneously, a second attacking group advanced in the Campo di Carne gorge, south of Cle Buon Riposo, to a line even with the first attack force. Enemy counterattacks on the group of houses were stopped by artillery fire. In addition, our artillery silenced five enemy batteries. Explosions were observed at four targets.

At 2000, the I Parachute Corps took over the sector of the 146th Grenadier Regiment; two artillery battalions of the 29th Panzer Grenadier Division were withdrawn.

Fourteenth Army ordered the 29th Panzer Grenadier Division to make a road reconnaissance on 29 February, for a possible attack at daybreak 1 March, the objective of which would be to occupy the Astura sector, between the road Borgo Podgora (G 045240) - Borgo Montello (F 976236) and the coast. This does not interfere with the original plan to employ the Division at the center of the LXXVI Panzer Corps' attack.

The Commanding General Fourteenth Army made the following report to the Commander in Chief Southwest:

"The divisions and regiments with little combat experience or insufficient training are not suited for difficult offensive operations. The 65th Infantry Division, 114th Jäger Division, and the 715th Motorized Infantry Division suffered heavy losses. Most casualties are inflicted by enemy artillery fire. Shell fragments are responsible for 75 percent of all wounds, while 10 to 15 percent of the casualties have been caused by enemy air attacks. The fact that due to insufficient training, the men do not know how to handle themselves properly in battle, has increased our casualties. The planning for attacks, the redeployment of troops, and the offensive operations now take longer, due to heavy losses among officers and noncommissioned officers."

B. Intelligence Report

According to prisoners of war, the 1st Battalion 180th Infantry Regiment of the 45th Infantry Division (US) is located at the northeastern edge of the Vallicelle Grandi woods. On its left is the 179th Infantry Regiment. The 1st Duke of Wellington Regiment and 2d Foresters Regiment are employed in the front line, while the 1st King's Shropshire Light Infantry Regiment is in a reserve position. Replacements from Naples increased the strength of the companies to 150 men.

The enemy seems to have transferred his attention from the Aprilia sector to the Cisterna-Littoria sector.

C. Statistics

German losses: (less 114th Jäger Division and the 362d Infantry Division) 37 killed, 116 wounded, and 18 missing.

Allied losses: 135 prisoners (130 British, 5 Americans), and 2 tanks put out of commission.

A. Operations Report

At 0400, the LXXVI Panzer Corps started the new attack against the beachhead with the 114th Jäger Division, 362d Infantry Division, 26th Panzer Division, and the Panzer Division "Hermann Göring".

The enemy had been pinned down and confused as to our intentions by I Parachute Corps' raids and local attacks along the entire front. Over one hundred prisoners were taken during these operations.

It was difficult to bring up the units of the LXXVI Panzer Corps to their initial positions, due to mud from the continuous rains. The attacks of the divisions, especially the 362d Infantry Division and 26th Panzer Division, were hampered as their troops were exhausted from marching in the mud. The attack was limited to local penetrations of the enemy's main line of resistance, because the defense area was stubbornly defended and strengthened by mines and barbed wire entanglements. The employment of tanks by the 362d Infantry Division was not possible, as the ground conditions were unfavorable. The 26th Panzer Division was unable to employ its tanks fully, because the Ponte Rotto bridge (F 997314) had been destroyed.

Several attacks of the 362d Infantry Division against the Cle del Pozzo, 2 km east of Cle Carano (F 940309), were unsuccessful in spite of a concentration of all forces. Raids by the 741st Jäger Regiment of the 114th Jäger Division wiped out two strongpoints in the area west of Torre di Padiglione (F 921289), and brought back 10 prisoners. Several attacks on Cle Carano (F 940309) were repulsed by strong defensive fire. Six tanks were lost during these attacks.

The right flank of the 26th Panzer Division, after crossing its own main line of resistance, was stopped by strong enemy resistance with very high losses. The 9th Panzer Grenadier Regiment on the left flank, attacked along the road running southwest from Ponte Rotto. After clearing mine fields on both sides of the road, it advanced and captured the crossroads, 1 km southwest of Ponte Rotto at 1230. Supported by tanks, it made several attempts to capture Hill 77 , 1.5 km west of Ponte Rotto, suffering heavy losses in officers and tanks; it was unsuccessful. The attack to seize the adjacent Rubbia Heights was halted by heavy fire.

Units of the Panzer Division "Hermann Göring" reached the line, 300 meters southeast of Isola Bella (G 006294), to S. Alberto (1 km southeast of Isola Bella), to benchmark 43 1.5 km southeast of Isola Bella. The right flank of the Division made little progress due to strong enemy resistance. At 1200, several tanks reached the north edge of Isola Bella.

The 715th Infantry Division sent assault troops to take the crossings over the Fosso di Cisterna, 3.5 km north of Borgo Podgora (G 045240), and the Mussolini Canal, 1 km north of Borgo Podgora. These assaults met strong enemy resistance, and did not reach their desired objectives. During the evening, the enemy pushed back our advanced positions to the old line of resistance at the left flank of the Division.

During the night, the sector of the I Parachute Corps had been heavily attacked by enemy artillery fire, which had increased before our attack began. Apparently, the enemy believed our main effort was going to be in this area. Our deception appeared to have been successful. However, enemy artillery was regrouped during the day, after which concentrated fire was laid in front of our attacking forces.

Fire from all of our artillery positions, supported by anti-aircraft and rocket fire at the points of main effort, was directed at enemy strongholds, pockets of resistance, and flank positions. Our artillery subjected the enemy's supply lines, assembly and unloading areas, mainly in the sector of Casale Campomorto (F 941270) and Le Ferriere (F 963242) to harassing fire throughout the entire day. Our counterbattery fire was successful in neutralizing the enemy's artillery. The enemy's rear area was subjected to constant shelling with all available long-range guns. Several direct hits on ships were observed. One ship was sunk in the harbor entrance to Anzio.

We aim to prevent the enemy from transferring troops from the front of the I Parachute Corps. Strong raids will be made on this front. It is also necessary that the LXXVI Panzer Corps establish one or more bridgeheads across the Astura as soon as possible. Combat teams supported by tanks will make the attack. The 29th Panzer Grenadier Division is transferred to the LXXVI Panzer Corps for employment on the east flank of the attacking force.

German Artillery Employed on the Beachhead

Number of Pieces	Type of Weapon	Caliber
151	howitzer	10.5 cm
61	howitzer	15 cm
46	guns	10 cm
8	light guns	7.5 cm
12	guns (Russian)	7.62 cm
18	guns	17 cm
12	heavy howitzers (Italian)	
20	captured enemy guns	
3	howitzers	21 cm
9	howitzers (French)	22 cm
2	railway guns	21 cm
51	rocket projectors	15 cm
7	rocket projectors	21 cm
	39 AA batteries	8.8 cm
Total: 400		

Allied artillery ammunition expenditure was 66,500 rounds, while the German artillery ammunition consumption was 1,183 tons, of which the following number of rounds were expended by the weapons indicated: Rocket projectors (15 cm) 817 rounds, rocket projectors (21 cm) 144 rounds, guns (17 cm) 600 rounds, and railway guns (21 cm) 12 rounds.

B. Intelligence Report

Enemy Information: According to prisoner of war reports, Company L, 3d Battalion 7th Infantry Regiment of the 3d Infantry Division (US) was in the area southwest of Colle del Pozzo 2 km west of Cle Carano (F 940309).

C. Statistics

German losses (minus 362d Infantry Division): 143 killed, 429 wounded, and 269 missing. Allied losses: 180 prisoners and 3 airplanes downed.

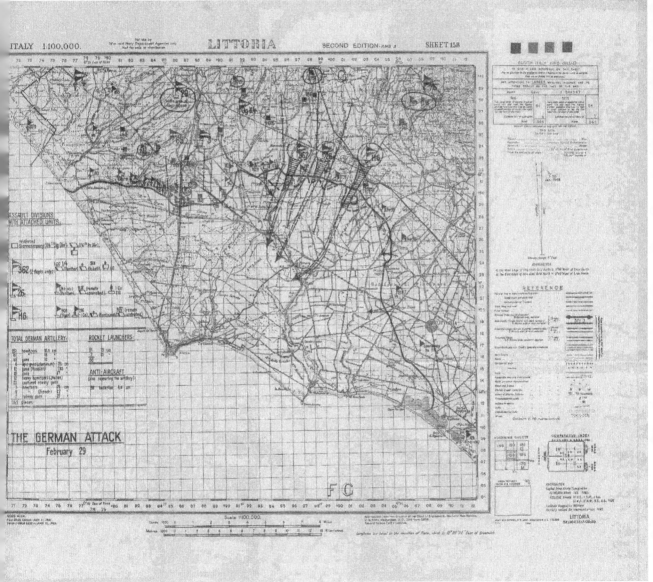

A. Operations Report

Operations, to harass the enemy by raids along the entire front of the I Parachute Corps, were continued. After the enemy received reinforcements, he attacked all important sectors of the LXXVI Panzer Corps. The Corps was forced to give up part of the ground gained the previous day.

At daybreak, the enemy made an attack on the 362nd Infantry Division, in the course of which he reached the Fosso di Carano (F 940309) and seized Hill 63, 800 meters northwest of Colle del Pozzo (F964312). We regained the height in a counterattack. An enemy assault at the Colle del Pozzo was halted by our artillery fire. The enemy forced the 26th Panzer Division to withdraw from the Rubbia Woods (F 984313), which we had taken in the morning. Due to enemy attacks and heavy casualties, the Panzer Division "Hermann Göring" lost the ground gained the day before.

The following order from Marshal Kesselring was received:

"Today's (20 February) successes did not meet our expectations, despite the fact that we had achieved surprise, that enemy artillery fire was light, and his air raids delayed.

Again and again, I have noticed an overestimate of the enemy. This has resulted in lack of aggressiveness by both officers and men. We are all aware that the importance of this attack is not only confined to this theater of war. However, we will succeed, only if officers and men regain their former self confidence as in olden days, inspired by an impetuous urge to attack.

It is necessary to keep on pushing forward even if adjacent troops have been stopped, and enemy strongpoints have to be bypassed. We must continue attempting to establish bridgeheads across the Mussolini Canal and the Astura Creek."

The Commanding General of the Fourteenth Army reported to the Commander in Chief Southwest that the failure, of the previous day, was mainly due to the deficiencies enumerated on 27 February, which are: insufficient training of troops, and young replacements, who are not qualified to meet the Allied troops in battle. Due to this, the Army will be unable to wipe out the beachhead with the troops on hand. The tactics which have been employed, viz. to reduce the beachhead gradually by concentrated attacks by several divisions, cannot effectively be continued much longer. New tactics must be employed, in order to enable us to meet the eventual enemy large-scale attack from the beachhead with an adequate number of troops and materiel. This attack will probably be made in connection with an offensive against the Tenth Army and, possibly, simultaneously with the main invasion in Western Europe if the weather conditions turn for the better. It will be the mission of the Army to harass the enemy and to keep him in the dark concerning our intentions, and to improve our positions in order to reduce the beachhead so as to place us in a favorable position to counter the eventual major enemy attack.

A message was sent from the Commander in Chief Southwest to the Commanding General Fourteenth Army at 1840. This message stated that contrary to the weather predictions, it has been raining continuously for 18 hours. The ground is so muddy that neither tanks nor horse-drawn vehicles can be moved. Therefore, all concentrated attacks must be halted. The divisions will continue to mount carefully-

prepared local raids. Units which are not needed for these
actions will be withdrawn for rest and replacements.

Order from Fourteenth Army to subordinate units

Since the attack on the 29 February did not lead to
the desired result, our next operation will be to launch
minor well-prepared attacks to push our lines forward and
to reduce the enemy beachhead. The 26th Panzer Division
and the 29th Panzer Grenadier Division will be withdrawn
from the front as tactical reserve.

In general, the orders to the Corps were to engage
the enemy along the entire front. At least two raids a
night will be launched in every division-sector. Attacks,
in company to battalion strength, will be carried out with
the twofold purpose of improving our positions and inflic-
ting heavy losses on the enemy; the objectives for attacks
will be chosen with those points in mind. These actions
will start immediately. Especially selected and equipped
assault companies or battalions will be formed in all divisions. Recent days have shown that the different arms
are not cooperating sufficiently in battle. It is imperative
that during the coming attacks mistakes be pointed out to
the troops, so that they will learn from experience. After
the attacks, the newly occupied lines will be fortified and
mined immediately to prevent effective enemy counteraction.
These preparations must not lower the spirit of aggressiveness. On the contrary, they should only be considered as
an aid for the continuance of our offensive operations.

In the sector of the I Parachute Corps it is most important to gain ground on the western flank of the 4th Parachute Division, in order to further reduce the beachhead in
this sector. It will be necessary to push forward the main
line of resistance to the Buon Riposo and Botaccia gorges.
To achieve this, the Corps will make attacks, in company to
battalion strength, on 2, 4, and 6 March. On each of these
days one attack will be made.

In the sector of the LXXVI Panzer Corps, the front must
be pushed forward, particularly in our current offensive sec-
tor. Possible objectives for these operations are Cle Bia-
daretto (F 918307), Cle Carano, Colle del Pozzo, the Rubbia
Woods and the Rubbia hill, Isola Bella, and the little woods
1 km northeast of Isola Bella. The 29th Panzer Grenadier
Division will be withdrawn as soon as possible. The 26th
Panzer Division will withdraw in the near future. The 29th
Panzer Grenadier Division will move to the area Cisterna-
Velletri, and the 26th Panzer Division will move to the area
Cecchina-Genzano-Albano. Both of these divisions will become
Fourteenth Army Reserve.

The mission of the artillery, including antiaircraft is
to support the offensive operations of the Corps, shell the
enemy artillery systematically, annihilate all observed enemy
points of resistance, fire on all profitable moving targets,
and shell enemy ships, harbor installations, and disembarkation
points.

Beginning 2 March, the following tank forces of the 69th
Panzer Regiment, which have been attached to the LXXVI Panzer
Corps, will be brought to their original assembly areas south-
ward and eastward of Rome: 301st Panzer Battalion (radio controlled demolition vehicles), 508th Tiger Battalion (including
a company of Ferdinand tanks), 1st Battalion 4th Panzer Regiment (Panther tanks), and the 216th Panzer Battalion.

The I Parachute Corps and the LXXVI Panzer Corps will form the following alert-units to be ready to move within 2 or 4 hours, in order to reinforce the units employed in coastal defense, in case of a possible enemy landing in the area of Civitavecchia: one company of the 60th Motorized Engineer Battalion, one company of the 22nd Airforce Engineer Battalion, one Panther tank company, one company of the 1st Antiaircraft Battalion, 12th Regiment, one company of the 590th GHQ Tank Destroyer Battalion, and infantry reserves as the condition demands (at present 145th Grenadier Regiment and 1 battalion 71st Motorized Grenadier Regiment).

B. Intelligence Report

The GHQ Tank Battalion 4th Queens Own Hussars (Br) is reemployed in the Campo di Carne sector, according to a captured map.

Further attacks against our advanced points must be expected.

C. Statistics

German losses: 202 killed, 707 wounded, and 465 missing.

Allied losses: 132 prisoners (66 British and 66 Americans), several machine guns, 1 truck and 1 radio set captured.

Tanks and self propelled guns fit for combat:

	Available evening 28 February	Available evening 1 March
Hornets	25	29
Tanks	165	147
Tigers	(32)	(14)
Panthers	(53)	(53)
Assault Howitzers	29	21
Assault Guns	46	58
Ferdinands	11	3

XXXVIII. 2 - 4 March 1944

A. Operations Report

Due to strong enemy counterattacks, one company of the 4th Parachute Division, which had occupied the eastern part of the Ciocca gorge (F 820305), was wiped out by the enemy. The group of houses, 1 km southwest of Ponte Rotto (F 997314), which had previously been taken by the 26th Panzer Division, had to be abandoned after a struggle of several days. In the course of this struggle, the houses changed hands several times.

In other sectors, scouting and raiding were the only activities. Enemy artillery fire has been generally light. However, during the morning of 2 March the enemy brought the sectors of the 114th Jäger Division and the 362nd Infantry Division under an artillery barrage.

During numerous heavy air raids on our rear areas and artillery positions, the enemy systematically neutralized our antiaircraft.

The following subjects were considered in a meeting of the Commander in Chief Southwest and the Commanding Generals of the armies: First, Marshal Kesselring believes that minor operations in the Mediterranean Theater, probably in Southern France, will precede the main invasion in Northern France. Nevertheless, heavy diversionary attacks at Livorno and Genoa are possible. Landing operations on the Adriatic coast are not likely at the present; the possibility of tactical landings at Pescara and Civitavecchia remains. Second, the mission of the Commander in Chief Southwest still is to defend central Italy and to reduce gradually the Nettuno beachhead. Third, the Fourteenth Army will transfer the following forces to the Tenth Army: 114th Jäger Division, one regiment before 20 March and the majority of the division by 25 March; 1st and 2nd Battalions of the 115th Motorized Grenadier Regiment, beginning on 8 March; 1st Battalion of the 71st Projector Regiment, formerly the Projector Demonstration Battalion, by 12 March; 450th Heavy Artillery Battalion, by 12 March; and the Panzer Division "Hermann Göring" to Group "von Zangen" for employment in the area of Livorno. The 3d Panzer Grenadier Division will get back from the Tenth Army the reinforced 8th Motorized Grenadier Regiment, by 8 March.

The German High Command intends to reinforce the Fourteenth Army with one railway battery (280 mm), and one Czechoslovakian railway battery (320 mm).

The Commander in Chief Southwest has ordered the immediate construction of a second line of defense ("C" line) from Macchia Idrovora (F 740343) in a northeasterly direction to the east coast. The line will be ready for occupancy, particularly in the threatened sector, by 30 April. The Fourteenth Army is responsible for the fortification from the west coast to the neighborhood of Artena.

On 3 March the Italian Marine Battalion "Barbarigo", consisting of Battalion Staff and four companies with strengths of 650 men, arrived at the 715th Infantry Division. It will be stationed in the area northeast of Littoria.

Army reserve: 29th Panzer Grenadier Division (less the elements currently employed in the front line) to be assembled in the area north of Velletri.

B. Intelligence Reports

The 2nd Company, 6th Queens Own, 169th Brigade 56th Infantry Division (Br), is located in the Michele gorge (F828315 to F845308) as confirmed by prisoners of war from Company C. The Battalion relieved the 10th Royal Berkshire Regiment on the 29 February. The 1st King's Shropshire Light Infantry (3rd Brigade 1st British Infantry Division) is now employed in the sector 1.5 km northwest of the road crossing Campo di Carne (F850890 to F270290). Prisoners of war state that Company C has been in this area for ten days.

The chart on page 79 shows estimated Allied ammunition expenditures for the period 16 February 1944 to 3 March 1944.

ALLIED ARTILLERY AMMUNITION EXPENDITURE

By Rounds for the Period 16 February to 3 March 1944

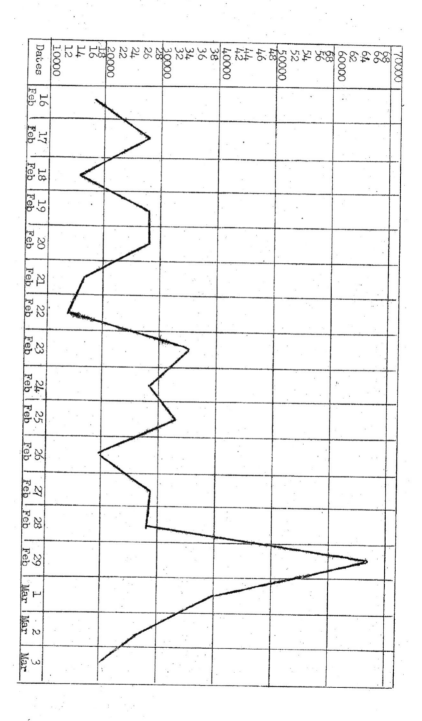

C. Statistics:

German losses: 156 killed, 667 wounded, and 209 missing.

Allied losses: 38 prisoners, 7 airplanes downed by anti-aircraft, several machine guns and small arms captured.

XXIX 5 to 9 MARCH 1944

A. Operations Report

During the entire period, combat and reconnaissance patrols were active on both sides.

Enemy bombing and strafing raids on 6 March against artillery emplacements in 362nd Infantry Division's sector met with no success. At 1200 on 6 March, the 26th Panzer Division took over the former sector of Panzer Division "Hermann Göring", which, in turn, was moved to Livorno, less its antiaircraft and armored units.

On 5 March, one company of Italian Marines, Battalion "Barbarigo", was committed in the sector of the 2nd Battalion of the 36th SS Panzer Grenadier Regiment, attached to 715th Infantry Division. This unit could not be employed for special missions because it lacked sufficient infantry training. The 114th Jäger Division, earmarked for mountain warfare on the southern front, will be equipped with mountain artillery.

On 7 March, the 114th Jäger Division's attack on the enemy stronghold at Cle Biadaretto, 2 km north of Cle Tre di Padiglione (F 921289), failed, due to the heavy barrage and the strongly defended and mined positions of the enemy.

During the night of 7 to 8 March 1944, enemy attacks against the 10th Parachute Regiment's right flank by about two companies, launched after two hours of artillery preparation, were repelled in hard fighting.

On 9 March, several enemy assaults, partly supported by tanks, launched at the boundary between the 65th Infantry Division and the 3rd Panzer Grenadier Division, were repulsed by determined counter-attacks.

Enemy artillery fire was very heavy, at times increasing to barrage pitch, especially along the Aprilia-Anzio highway and in the Cle Buon Riposo area (F854310). The enemy fired an extraordinary number of smoke shells. He also employed a new type of shell for the first time, which explodes about 150 meters from the ground, ejecting four smoke pots in different directions, that produce heavy smoke after hitting the ground some 50 meters apart.

Our artillery bombarded the enemy's strongpoints, positions, supply traffic and gun emplacements. Good results were observed in several cases. Long-range artillery, supported by antiaircraft artillery, bombed the harbor at Anzio. Two merchant vessels were hit, one of them pouring out great quantities of smoke. Violent explosions were also observed.

During the night of 8 to 9 March our air forces launched a heavy aerial attack on the Nettuno area.

The Commander in Chief Southwest foresees the possibility of major airborne and seaborne enemy landings in the very near future, coordinated with an offensive against the Tenth Army's front. The following reserves are available for the defense: 29th Panzer Grenadier Division (Fourteenth Army Reserve); Elements of 3rd Panzer Grenadier Division (I Parachute Corps); and the 26th Panzer Division (LXXVI Panzer Corps Reserve). These units will be on a two hour alert status from 2100 to 0300 daily. Reconnaissance for possible commitment in the Civitavecchia area was to be executed at once. The following units are subject to the same alert status: 3rd Battalion 2nd Artillery Demonstration Regiment; 1st Company 590th Anti-tank Battalion, 1st Battalion 4th Panzer Regiment (Panther tanks), and the 60th Engineer Battalion.

Repeated observations confirmed that the frequently erroneous release of our artillery barrages was due to the use of flare signals by the enemy. For this reason, flare signals changing daily, at noon, will be introduced immediately.

Dispersion and echelonment in depth of enemy artillery positions render our artillery's counter fire more difficult. To remove this obstacle, the Chief Artillery Officer, Fourteenth Army, requested the attachment of a howitzer battalion and a heavy flat-trajectory gun battalion (Schwere Flachfeuer-Abteilung).

The Commanding General, Fourteenth Army, reported to the Commander in Chief Southwest, that no suitable tunnels as air protection were available for the employment of the two railway artillery batteries promised by the German High Command. The tunnel, farthest to the south, gives an effective range of only 3 kilometers in front of our own main line of resistance. In case the batteries must operate from the tunnels, the Army will have to forego their employment.

Enemy fighter-bomber activity is continually causing considerable losses in motor vehicles. Considering the difficulty of replacing motor transport, Fourteenth Army again points out that all convoy traffic by day must be reduced to the minimum.

B. Intelligence Report

Prisoners of war report that the 40th Royal Marine Commando is established 1.5 km northwest of Fta Campo di Carne (F 862284). The Commandos, 800 men strong, had disembarked at Anzio on 3 March. During the night of 5 to 6 March, they relieved the 2nd Foresters. Same source stated that the 43rd Marine Commando (Br) who came ashore with the first wave on the bridgehead, were withdrawn to Naples several weeks ago. It was also established from prisoners of war that the 3rd Battalion 30th Infantry Regiment of the 3rd Infantry Division (US), is at Fossa della Pedata, 1 km west of Cle Carano (F 940309), and has occupied this position for the last ten days. The 7th Infantry Regiment 3rd Infantry Division (US), is newly established 1.5 km southwest of Ponte Rotto (F 997314). Prisoners taken belonged to the antitank platoon, the Headquarters Company, and the Engineer Company. The Regiment has occupied this position for the last two days. Lt. Gen. Truscott, previously commanding the 3rd Infantry Division (US), was transferred to the VI Corps, as Commanding General. General McDaniel is mentioned as the new commanding officer of the 3rd Infantry Division (US), with Col. Sherman as Chief of Staff.

There were no indications of the arrival of new units. Commitment of the 1st Armored Division (US) in the Cisterna sector (G 0232), is to be expected.

C. Statistics

German losses: 162 killes, 646 wounded, and 66 missing.

Allied losses: 27 prisoners, 2 tanks destroyed, 2 anti-tank guns destroyed, and 1 airplane downed.

XL 10 to 14 MARCH 1944

A. Operations Report

Shortly after midnight on the 14th March, the enemy attacked in battalion strength supported by tanks. The attack, which was directed against our positions west of the Aprilia-Anzio highway was turned back with heavy enemy losses. During the same night, two more attacks from the gorges Caronte (F 854297) and Campo di Carne, south of Cle Buon Riposo (F 859310), succeeded in making several penetrations. However, by immediate counterattacks, the original line was reestablished by early morning. Enemy raids were turned back on the entire beachhead front. Our reconnaissance and raid operations were successful in taking prisoners. One scouting party of 5 men succeeded in taking 36 prisoners.

Enemy artillery fire was comparatively light. Since the beginning of March, the enemy has extensively been employing artillery observation planes, especially in the area of Cisterna (G 0232), and south of Aprilia (F 875333). Our artillery firing white phosphorous shells, caused a fire in an enemy motor pool at Le Ferriere (F 963242), and our long range artillery shelled enemy supply traffic. It was observed that three transports were hit, and that several ships were forced to withdraw from their berths in the harbor.

Throughout the entire period there was considerable enemy air reconnaissance, and fighter-bombers were active. Our main defensive area and artillery positions were bombed and strafed. Fires were observed at Anzio and Nettuno after air raids.

On 13 March, in the Fourteenth Army sector, the remaining elements of the Panzer Division "Hermann Göring", consisting of antiaircraft regiments and Panzer regiments, were sent to the new operational area at Livorno. The staff of the 26th Panzer Regiment took over the command of the coastal sector of the LXXVI Panzer Corps, in the area of the 715th Infantry Division, and the 26th Panzer Reconnaissance Battalion was attached to the 715th Infantry Division in the area southeast of Littoria.

On 14 March, the 362nd Infantry Division relieved the 67th Panzer Grenadier Regiment and elements of the 2nd Battalion 9th Panzer Grenadier Regiment. The bulk of the 23th Panzer Division has now been taken from the front and made Army Reserves. One regimental group is in the area of Cori (G 095380) and another is in the area of Genzano - Velletri.

By order of the Commander in Chief, Southwest, the 29th Panzer Grenadier Division will move to the area south of Rome, between the Tiber and the Via Appia, as Army Group reserve.

Army Reserve is comprised of the staff of the 69th Panzer Regiment, with the following units: the 1st Battalion 4th Panzer Regiment, the 508th Heavy Panzer Battalion (Tiger tanks), the 653rd Heavy Tank Destroyer Battalion (Ferdinands), and the 216th Assault Howitzer Battalion.

During the present lull in the fighting, an opportunity has been given to improve deficiencies in close antitank combat techniques. Such training has been given; 13 officers, 73 non-commissioned officers, and 177 men have finished the course. The training is mainly concerned with the employment of rocket launchers (bazookas) and antitank grenades.

At the present, the divisions are equipped with the following:

Unit	Rocket Launchers (Bazookas)	Antitank Grenades
4th Parachute Jäger Division	25	200
65th Infantry Division	40	327
3rd Panzer Grenadier Division	12	336
362nd Infantry Division	59	180
26th Panzer Division	76	425
29th Panzer Grenadier Division	20	635
Total	232	2103

After Fourteenth Army was regrouped, it was possible to relieve the battalions in the line according to schedule. Of three battalions in a regiment, two stayed in position, and the third was sent to the rear area to rest and receive newly arrived replacements in its units. These battalions were also used to erect switchpositions in the rear. With this system, it was possible for each battalion to have approximately 10 days rest after having been at the front for three weeks. During this period, outstanding soldiers were given the opportunity to spend two days in Rome with hotel accommodations.

Personnel strength of the Fourteenth Army is depicted in the chart below:

Units	Officers	Enlisted men
Army troops		
Actual strength	3,711	101,466
Combat strength	1,632	50,113
Rear echelon troops of combat units	348	16,464
Supply troops	1,063	16,769

Air Force Ground troops		
Actual strength	779	25,018
Combat strength	400	12,896
Rear echelon troops of combat units	187	5,088
Supply troops	111	3,053

SS troops		
Actual strength	24	1,527
Combat strength	17	769
Rear echelon troops of combat units	1	232

Total strength		
Actual strength	4,514	128,011
Combat strength	2,049	63,778
Rear echelon troops		
of combat units	536	21,784
Supply troops	1,174	19,822

Other units	Officers and Enlisted Men
Italian units	2,129
Italian auxiliary supply units	248
Russian auxiliary supply units	655
Other auxiliary supply units	341
Total	3,373

B. Eyewitness Report

The enemy artillery observation planes which were in the
air every day, were harassing our troops, because each moving
object was at once fired upon. Night, was the only time that
commanders could make an inspection of the main line of resistance and get in touch with their men. The defense against
artillery observation planes was very difficult, because the
planes stayed about 500 meters from our main line of resistance.
Due to their maneuverability, they could not be followed by our
antiaircraft guns.

C. Intelligence Report

It has been learned from prisoners of war that the 6th
Seaforth 17th Brigade of the 5th Infantry Division (Br) is
in the Michele gorge (F 823315 to F 841310). The Battalion
came from Naples and landed at Anzio on 9 March. It relieved
parts of the 1st London Scots on 10 March. The strength of
each company is 110 men. One week ago, this Battalion was employed at Garigliano and later relieved by the Americans. After
5 days of rest south of Naples, it assembled, probably with the
entire 17th Brigade.

The 14th Foresters is in the Bottacia gorge. (vicinity of
F 854297) This battalion was employed in the Middle East and
came via Algiers and Naples to Anzio, where it landed on 20
February. It belonged to the 18th Independent Infantry Brigade
and consists of four infantry companies, a Heavy Company, and a
Headquarters Company. Its strength is approximately 600 men.
Companies A, B, and C are committed. The 9th King's Own York-
shire Light Infantry Buffs, strength unknown, and the 14th For-
esters, belong to the 18th Infantry Brigade. The 9th King's
Own Yorkshire Light Infantry landed at Anzio at the beginning of
March, after having been employed in Africa for 2 years. On 7
March they relieved the 1st King's Shropshire Light Infantry
310th Brigade of the 1st Infantry Division (Br). The 5th and
51st Infantry Divisions (Br) are probably in England.

The 1st Ranger Battalion of the 1st Special Service Force is
1 km east of Isola Bella (G 006294), according to captured documents.

The heavy traffic in the area south of Aprilia is probably
due to the arrival of the 5th Infantry Division (Br).

D. Statistics

German losses: 121 killed, 372 wounded, 65 missing.

Allied losses: 173 prisoners (163 British), 20 machine guns, and 140 small arms captured.

XLI The German Command's Mid-March Estimate of the Situation And German Intentions

A. Enemy Situation, according to report of 13 March 1944 from Fourteenth Army to Commander in Chief Southwest.

After our major attacks were discontinued in the beginning of March, the enemy has shown increased activity. His frequent reconnaissance and combat patrols have the twofold task of procuring intelligence and concealing regroupments; lately these patrols have also taken place in the Littoria area.

In addition to replacements for depleted units the following new units have been brought up to the beachhead: 40th Royal Marine Commando, elements of 17th Brigade of the 5th Infantry Division (Br), and the 14th Foresters.

From the western flank to Borgo Podgora the defensive positions are well fortified and manned at all times. The bulk of reserves, estimated at ten to eleven British infantry battalions and six to eight American battalions, is believed to be in the area south of Aprilia. There, the enemy places his main emphasis both for the offensive as well as the defensive; his secondary emphasis lies in the region southwest of Cisterna. A local attack in the Littoria sector aiming to force the German artillery positions further away from disembarkation points appears to be possible.

As yet we have no knowledge of a specific date for an Allied offensive. Such offensive action is to be expected in combination with major strategic operations and an attack on the southern front. The enemy continued to reorganize his forces as evidenced by the relief of front units. The enemy's knowledge of weakened German forces must have strengthened his intentions for an offensive on the beachhead.

B. Enemy order of battle, as given by the intelligence officer Fourteenth Army.

VI Corps (US)   under Fifth Army Command
1st Special Service Forces Brigade (US)
504th Parachute Regiment of the 82nd Airborne Division (US)
3rd Infantry Division (US)
509th Parachute Battalion (US)
751st Tank Battalion (US)
1st and 3rd Ranger Battalions (US)
23rd Tank Brigade (Br)
Tank Battalion "Greys" (Br)
1st Armored Division (US)
45th Infantry Division (US)
Tank Battalion (4th Hussars) (Br)
1st Infantry Brigade (Br)
18th Infantry Brigade (Br)
5th Infantry Division (Br)
56th Infantry Division (Br)
191st Tank Battalion (US)
36th Engineer Regiment (US)
4th Ranger Battalion (US)

C. German Intentions

As the 114th Jäger Division has been transferred to the Tenth Army and the Panzer Division "Hermann Göring" has been withdrawn to the area of Livorno, the German Command cannot plan a major attack for the elimination of the beachhead within the near future. German divisions are battle weary and have suffered considerable losses. The following effective combat strength was reported by General Hartmann of the German Army High Command, after his visit to the front on 4 to 6 March: 65th Infantry Division, consisting of 145th and 147th Infantry Regiments, 2,680 men; 114th Jäger Division, 4,582 men; 1028th Panzer Grenadier Regiment, 1,218 men; and the 715th Infantry Division, 3,099 men. This gave a total of 11,579 men.

Our artillery is weakened considerably. Statistics of 15 March show the following ready for action:

Type of Weapon	Calibre	Number of Pieces
Artillery:		
Light Artillery:		
Guns	up to 99 mm	
Howitzers	up to 129 mm	158
Medium artillery:		
Guns	100-209 mm	
Howitzers	130-209 mm	
Howitzers (Mörser)	210-249 mm	99
Heavy-Superheavy:		
Guns	210 mm and up	
Howitzers	210 mm and up	
Howitzers (Mörser)	250 mm and up	2
Rocket Projectors:		
Medium	110-159 mm	24
Heavy	160-219 mm	18
Antiaircraft artillery:		
Light	up to 36 mm	419
Medium	37-59 mm	35
Heavy	60-159 mm	140

Transportation difficulties often delay the arrival of ammunition allotments.

The enemy regrouped his artillery pulling back emplacement positions. Therefore, the range of our howitzers and antiaircraft guns is too short to reach enemy artillery positions, and only the few 100 mm guns at our disposal can do so.

Number of tanks and assault guns as of 24 March.	Pz III (50mm)	Pz IV (75mm)	Pz V (Panther)	Pz VI (Tiger)	Flame thrower	Assault guns
216th Assault Pz Bn						35
26th Panzer Division	5	51			7	
29th Panzer Gren Div	8	18				
3rd Panzer Gren Div						25
1st Bn 4th Pz Regt			40			
508th Pz Bn				32		
Assault Gun Bn XI Airforce Corps						17 (Italian)
Total	13	69	40	32	7	77

Due to their weakened condition the forces employed in the front line cannot be considered fit for any major attack at this time. Only the 26th Panzer Division and the 29th Panzer Grenadier Division are capable of any large scale operations. Both units presently constitute the Army Group Reserve, located south of Rome. Tank units, attached to the staff of the 69th Panzer Regiment with the exception of the Panther Battalion are brought into forward positions as a countermeasure against tank supported attacks of the enemy. Two groups are formed: First, "Group West" in the area of Clo Campoleone (F 860406), composed of two companies of Tiger tanks and one company of assault guns. Second, "Group East", between Genzano and Velletri, consisting of one company of Tiger tanks, two companies of assault guns, and one company of heavy self-propelled antitank guns.

Since the German units are considerably weakened and the enemy is constantly fortifying his positions, the German command can only plan a gradual reduction of the beachhead. An order dated 16 March from the German Army High Command emphasized this fact, as follows: "....we must continue to attack in the Nettuno sector, in order to keep the initiative. Attacks must be made continuously in small sectors so that the beachhead is steadily reduced....We have experienced in the past that our failures were due mainly to enemy artillery. Further attacks must be executed according to the tactics of the Ludendorff offensive in 1918."

Fourteenth Army will receive 12 howitzers (210 mm), seven batteries of 122 mm - 152 mm guns, from Germany, two batteries of 210 mm guns from artillery reserve France, and one railway artillery battery of 320 mm guns. The ammunition supply will be increased even though it means reducing rations. Part of the required food is to be procured locally.

On 13 March, the Commanding General Fourteenth Army recommended to Army Group the following two plans for attack, either of which can be put into effect after 29 March, provided the ground has dried. First, attack against the northern flank of the beachhead with the objective of gaining the line, Buon Riposo gorge 2 km south Clo Buon Riposo (F 859310) - crossroads Cantoniera (F 863282) - south edge of wood Vallicelle Grandi, 2 km west of Tre di Padigliano (F921289) .5 km north of Tre di Padiglione - Clo Savrini (F 920296) - Clo Carano (F 940309). The attack is to be carried out in three limited assaults. Secondly, an attack with the objective of gaining the line; bench mark 67, group of houses 1 km southwest of Ponte Rotto (F 997314) - bench mark 60, on hill with windmill 1 km west - northwest of Isola Bella (G 006294) - Isola Bella Borgo Podgora (G 045240). A successful outcome of this attack will assist further action to establish bridgeheads across the Mussolini Canal and an eventual breakthrough to the Astura.

Both attacks would involve the commitment of the 26th and 29th Divisions now in Army Group Reserve. If the latter plan is executed, it is feared that one of the assault divisions will have to be committed to hold the newly captured ground. In addition, the Fourteenth Army is confronted with the following problems: First, enemy landings may occur at Terracina (codeword "Thea"); between the front line of the I Parachute Corps and the mouth of the Tiber (codeword "Rückendeckung"); and the coastal defense sector Cecina - Mouth of the Tiber (codeword "Caecilie"). Detailed orders were issued concerning the fortification of the coastal defense sectors, the plan for tactical countermeasures, and the organization of alert units in case of enemy airborne operations. The 92nd Infantry Division which is in activation is to defend the coast line from the mouth of the Tiber to the boundary of the Fourteenth Army at Cecina. Secondly, due to the lack of safety in Rome, strict orders concerning entrance into the city limits are issued. Rome has been declared an "Open City" and all service units will be moved outside the city. Only medical and quartermaster units which operate bakeries, butcher shops, tailor shops, etc., will remain. Thirdly, the partisans, consisting of communists, Badoglio followers, and prisoners of war at large, endanger the areas south of Perugia and east of Orvisto. The 103rd Reconnaissance Battalion has been dispatched to these areas.

XLII 15 - 19 MARCH 1944

A. Operations Report

Particularly at night, during this period, routine reconnaissance and raiding activities took place.

Early on 15 March, the Allies captured the strongpoint at K 9, 1.5 km southeast of Tre Spaccasassi (F 917330), with overwhelming forces. Despite a counterattack, during which we suffered heavy losses, the group of houses could not be retaken.

Withdrawal of the 26th Panzer Division was completed on 15 March. The 362nd Infantry Division took over this sector. The 26th Panzer Division will be assembled as Army Reserve, in the area directly west of Velletri.

The relief of the 114th Jäger Division by the 1028th Panzer Grenadier Regiment began on 13 March, and will be completed by 20 March. On 19 March, the present sector of the 114th Jäger Division will be taken over by the 3rd Panzer Grenadier Division (I Parachute Corps).

On 18 March, our assault troops succeeded in penetrating enemy positions in the wooded area at the Moletta gorge (F 813313). Infantry weapons were captured. The enemy had considerable losses and his position was destroyed.

At 0730, 19 March, after very heavy artillery preparatory fire which extended to the Cisterna sector (G 0232), the enemy attacked at several points southwest of Aprilia (F 875333). These attacks were continued throughout the day, at times in battalion strength. They were repulsed partly by close combat and partly by immediate counterattacks. Forty-five prisoners were taken.

B. Intelligence Report

It has been learned from prisoners of war that the 36th Combat Engineer Regiment is located south of Torre della Moletta (F 774312). The 1st Battalion of this regiment is committed north of Highway 82; 2nd Battalion is in reserve; 3rd Battalion is located on the coast.

It also was learned from prisoners of war of B Company that the 2nd Cameronians (13th Brigade 5th Infantry Division (Br)) is located in the area west of Michele gorge (F 828315 to F 845308). It landed at Anzio on 12 March, and is replacing the 56th Infantry Division (Br). On 14 March, part of the Queen's Royal Regiment was relieved. A and C Companies of this unit have not as yet been committed. In the morning of 19 March, the 46th Tank Battalion (Br), attached to 1st Infantry Division (Br), took part in an attack west of the Aprilia-Anzio Highway. E and G Companies 30th Infantry Regiment of the 3rd Infantry Division (US) are committed on both sides of Cle Carano (F 940309). The 1st Battalion is held in reserve.

Continuous convoy activity was observed in the harbor area
of Anzio-Nettuno with a daily average of 30 to 40 units, including
LST's, transports, several large freighters, tankers, destroyers,
and escort vessels.

By smoke screens, the enemy tried to conceal the reorganization
and replacement of his troops. The enemy seems to be preparing further
attacks.

C. Statistics

German losses: 150 killed, 646 wounded, 76 missing.

Allied losses: 78 prisoners, 2 tanks put out of commission,
2 planes downed by antiaircraft, and heavy and light infantry
weapons captured.

XLIII. 20 - 24 MARCH 1944

A. Operations Report

On the front, the only activity was scouting and raiding. Reconnaissance patrols reported the construction of new barbed-wire
entanglements by the enemy. For this reason, raids by both sides
were rather unsuccessful. During the mopping up of the Michele
gorge near Appolonia (F 828314) on 20 March, 35 British dead were
found. Their small arms, machine guns, and mortars were brought
in.

The artillery continued the usual harassing fire on recognized
objectives. The enemy ammunition expenditure was much larger than
ours. After our artillery shelled the enemy rear areas, explosions
and fires were observed. It was assumed that large ammunition dumps
were hit. Our long-range artillery fired on ships lying in the harbor of Anzio-Nettuno, and occasional direct hits were observed.

B. Intelligence Report

It has been learned from prisoners of war that the 2nd Camer-
onians 13th Brigade of the 5th Infantry Division (Br) was in the
Michele gorge (F 823315 to F 845308), and was replaced by the 2nd
Battalion Inniskillings 13th Brigade of the 5th Infantry Division
(Br) on 21 February. The 14th Foresters 18th Independent Infantry
Brigade (Br), is located 1 km north of the Campo di Carne cross-
road (F 862284).

Captured documents yielded the following information:

On the front is the 6th Seaforth 17th Brigade, in second line
the 2nd Wiltshire 13th Brigade; both of the 5th Infantry Division
(Br).

Documents taken from dead enemy soldiers revealed that the
1st Reconnaissance Battalion of the 1st Infantry Division (Br) is
stationed in the sector northeast of Campo di Carne. (F 850270 to
F 890270).

Daily disembarkations of reinforcements for the beachhead have
been observed. On 21 March, for the first time, enemy propaganda leaflets were shot into our lines at Cisterna (G 0232); on the following

days this also happened in other sectors. In several sectors white phosphorous shells were used by the enemy.

C. Statistics

German losses: 110 killed, 394 wounded, and 16 missing.

Allied losses: 8 prisoners, 1 tank put out of commission; 1 airplane downed, and small arms captured.

XLIV. 25 - 29 MARCH 1944

A. Operations Report

Raid, reconnaissance, and artillery activities continued on both sides. Combat patrols often clashed in no-man's land. Results were negligible and losses relatively high.

On the morning of 26 March, the enemy captured a German strongpoint north of the Rubbia forest, 1.5 km west of Ponte Rotto (F 997-314), with an attack in company strength. He was repulsed after hand-to-hand fighting.

The coastal defense sector north of Castiglione and west of Grosseto up to Cecina was separated from the Fourteenth Army.

In the sector of the 65th Infantry Division, the 165th Infantry Battalion was relieved by the 2nd Battalion 1027th Infantry Regiment on 28 March. In the sector of the 362nd Infantry Division, the 362nd Fusilier Battalion was relieved by elements of the 1028th Panzer Grenadier Division on 27 March. The 556th Ost Battalion was transferred to the 362nd Infantry Division and assigned to 955th Infantry Regiment as 3rd (Ost) Battalion. The 1st Battalion of the Italian Assault Brigade "Barbarigo" was assigned to 715th Infantry Division.

At noon on 29 March, Army Group issued codeword "Caecilia I", i.e., enemy landings are imminent in the Tarquinia-Civitavecchia area. Consequently, during the night, the 29th Panzer Grenadier Division was transferred from the assembly area, 12 km south of Rome, to the vicinity of Bracciano lake; only the 71st Panzer Grenadier Regiment remained.

B. Intelligence Report

Newly established: The 1st Green Howards 15th Brigade of the 5th Infantry Division (Br) is with Company D at Torre di Moletta (F 774312). On 24 March, this Battalion relieved the 3rd Battalion of the 36th Engineer Regiment (US). The 2nd Royal Inniskilling Fusiliers 13th Brigade of the 5th Infantry Division (Br), committed on 21 March, was relieved by the 2nd Royal Scots Fusiliers 17th Brigade of the 5th Infantry Division (Br) on the 27 March. This Battalion landed at Anzio with 2 other battalions of the 17th Brigade, viz. the 2nd Northamptonshire and the 6th Seaforth Highlanders) on 12 March.

On the 14 March, the 2nd Battalion of the Royal Scots Fusiliers and the 2nd Battalion of Northamptonshire Regiment were attached as reserve to the 40th Royal Marine Commando. The 6th Seaforth, on the left of the 40th Royal Marine Commando, was withdrawn from the frontline. Company strength was 60 men. In the southern sector of the

Riserva Nuova gorge, 1 km southwest Cle Buon Riposo (F 859310), one prisoner belonging to the 1st King's Shropshire Light Infantry 3rd Brigade of the 1st Infantry Division (Br) was taken. On 23 March, Company C of this battalion relieved parts of the 1st King's Own Yorkshire Light Infantry 15th Brigade of the 5th Infantry Division (Br).

On 26 March, for the first time, elements of the newly arrived 34th Infantry Division (US) were identified. According to statements by prisoners of war, the 2nd Battalion 168th Infantry Regiment of the 34th Infantry Division (US) was transferred 6 days ago from Naples to Anzio. Two days ago the Battalion with a company strength of 200 men each was committed in the Isola Bella area (G 006294) which was the original sector of the 15th Infantry Regiment of the 3rd Infantry Division (US).

Documents from dead enemy soldiers revealed that the 2nd and 3rd Battalion 7th Infantry Regiment of the 3rd Infantry Division (US) were stationed in the sector 1.5 km west of Ponte Rotto (F 997-314).

According to statements of two prisoners from Company L the position of the 3rd Battalion 168th Infantry Regiment of the 34th Infantry Division (US) was established north of the Mussolini Canal in the former sector of the 2nd Battalion 504th Parachute Regiment. The 504th Parachute Regiment was supposed to have been withdrawn and replaced by elements of the 34th Infantry Division (US). Prisoners stated that the Fosso Carano (F 955328 to F 940310) is the boundary between the 45th and 34th Infantry Division.

In the harbor area of Anzio-Nettuno, heavy shipping traffic (a daily average of 50 to 60 units) has been observed.

Because of the drying up of the terrain and the appearance of the 34th Infantry Division (US) on the beachhead, it can be assumed that the enemy intends an attack presumably in a northerly direction.

D. Statistics

German losses: 93 killed, 397 wounded, and 32 missing.

Allied losses: 17 prisoners, infantry arms captured, 3 barrage balloons shot down over Anzio, and 2 ammunition dumps destroyed by direct hits.

XLV. 30 MARCH - 3 APRIL 1944

A. Operations Report

Patrol activity continued on both sides. Enemy outpost positions on the north side of the Michele gorge (F 824315 to F 841310), were captured by our scouting parties on 31 March, and held against strong enemy counterattacks.

The main line of resistance in the sector of the 3rd Panzer Grenadier Division southwest of Aprilia was considered a disadvantageous position in case of large scale enemy attacks. For that reason, it was strengthened in depth, while the main line of resistance was held with reduced forces. On 30 March, we succeeded in destroying the bridge 1.5 km southwest of Borgo Piave (G 053203) with remote-controlled demolition vehicles (Goliath). Thirteen prisoners were taken.

There was the usual artillery activity with occasional surprise barrages. Long-range artillery employed in shelling disembarkation points, ran short of ammunition at the end of the month. In the beginning of April, the ammunition supply was replenished. Shelling was resumed and hits were observed.

The 1st Battalion 4th Panzer Regiment (Panther Tanks), less the 1st Company which remained in the Cassino sector, was shifted to Pratica di Mare (F 735410), to replace the 29th Panzer Grenadier Division.

Terrain conditions were so poor that they were comparable only with the mud on the Russian front, during the worst period of the year. The level of surface water continued to rise. On 23 March, it was decided that the attack planned for 29 March would have to be postponed for several days, because of terrain conditions and the difficulty of ammunition supply. The Army now ordered the preparation for an offensive from the east, to reduce the beachhead. An attack of this kind was thought to be more promising, particularly in the Borgo Podgora sector (Sossano) (G 045240) - Borgo Piave (G 053204). The aim was to thrust across the Mussolini Canal toward the Astura. On the second day, to execute a flanking thrust from the south against the enemy positions in front of Cisterna (G 0232). However, for the latter action, a third assault division is required.

A Fourteenth Army summary concerning the fighting qualities of its units gave the following estimates: Units falling into Combat Quality Classification I are the 3d Panzer Grenadier Division, 26th Panzer Division, 29th Panzer Grenadier Division, Infantry Demonstration Regiment, and General Headquarters Panzer and Antitank Battalions. Those falling into Classification II are the 4th Paratroop Division, 362d Infantry Division, 1027 Panzer Grenadier Regiment, and the 1028 Panzer Grenadier Regiment. Combat Classification III consists of the 715th Infantry Division, 92d Infantry Division (in activation).

Attached Italian units were evaluated as follows: (1) Paratroop Battalion "Nembo", (2) Battalion "Barbarigo", and (3) 1st Battalion Italian Assault Brigade.

Comparison of Artillery Strength: With his units up to full strength, the enemy has on the beachhead more than 442 artillery pieces, not including antiaircraft artillery, compared to our 323 pieces, only 226 of which were ready for action on 31 March. Even if we include the 109 antiaircraft guns and the 61 rocket launchers, whose ammunition supply is limited, the Allies would still have a numerical superiority of 46 pieces, excluding the artillery of the 34th Infantry Division (US), which is in transit.

B. Intelligence Report

Prisoners of war reveal that the 1st York and Lancaster Battalion of the 5th Infantry Division (Br) is in the area west of the Ciocca gorge (F 853310). A prisoner of war confirmed that the 9th Kings Own Yorkshire Light Infantry of the 18th Infantry Brigade (Br) is south of Cle Buon Riposo (F 853310).

The 24th Guard Infantry Brigade is said to have been sent to Naples for a rest period. They are expected to return on 4 April to relieve the 18th Independent Brigade (Br).

The Allied relief schedule is : 10 days front-line, 2 days 2d line, 6 days rest.

Along the canal, cigarette packages were found, which exploded when opened.

C. Statistics

German losses: 147 killed, 420 wounded, and 12 missing.

Allied losses: 29 prisoners and small arms captured.

XLVI. 4 - 8 APRIL 1944

A. Operations Report

No activity except the usual patrols. A derelict enemy vessel (LCA) with two machine guns was brought in, north of the mouth of the Tiber.

The enemy artillery was somewhat more active. His surprise fire often increased to heavy barrage fire, especially in the area of Ardea (F 787350) and Cisterna (G 0232). 18 cm guns with a high burst effect were observed in the northern sector. Explosions and fires were seen after our artillery fired on enemy rear areas and landing places. It is assumed that large enemy dumps were located there.

Air activity was heavy. Fighter units of 15 to 24 planes repeatedly attacked artillery, antiaircraft artillery positions, and traffic centers.

Due to strongly fortified positions and the alertness of enemy troops, surprise raids in force were nearly impossible. The raids that were made resulted in heavy casualties and had little success. On 7 April 1944, the Army ordered such raids to be prepared very thoroughly and to be supported by heavy artillery fire, even at the expense of the element of surprise. Reconnaissance patroling was to be continued, in order to have a clear picture of the enemy situation at all times.

The 216th Assault Tank Battalion, with 15 cm assault howitzers, was transferred to the area Pisa - Lucca as Army Group Reserve.

On 7 April, after operations against partisans south of Perugia were completed, the 103d Reconnaissance Battalion relieved the 129th Reconnaissance Battalion in the area west of Terracina.

B. Intelligence Report

Prisoners of war state that the 2d Battalion Stafford 2d Brigade of the 1st Infantry Division (Br) is now in the new operational area north of Highway 82 at (F 876285).

The 133d 135th, and 168th Infantry Regiments of the 34th Infantry Division (US) are now on the beachhead and in action.

Artillery ammunition expenditure is estimated at 51,000 rounds.

The enemy fired propaganda leaflets into our lines. A new type of shell was observed in the east sector. The shell exploded 50 meters above the ground and broke into 3 smaller shells which left green smoke trails.

Due to less naval and ground activity on the beachhead, and increased artillery fire on our command posts and observation posts, it is assumed that enemy preparations for the attack have been completed.

C. Statistics

German losses: 140 killed, 421 wounded, and 18 missing.

Allied losses: 20 prisoners, machine guns and small arms captured, 1 tank put out of commission.

XLVII. 9 - 13 April 1944

A. Operations Report

Continued reconnoitering took place during this period. During the night 13 April, six sudden artillery concentrations, using all artillery and antiaircraft artillery at the disposal of the Fourteenth Army, were directed at enemy rear areas and particularly at identified ammunition and fuel dumps approximately 8 km north of Nettuno. At the same time enemy antiaircraft artillery positions were shelled in order to protect our participating aircraft.

All convoy traffic south of the line Piombino - Ancona has been suspended during daylight hours because of the losses inflicted by enemy fighter-bombers.

Army Group ordered on 9 April, that the 26th Panzer Division be moved to the area between Nemi Lake and Segni, to act as Army Group Reserve, available for the central Italian front also. Elements of this division were utilized during the day to consolidate the C-Line. However, the 93d Artillery Regiment of the 26th Panzer Division and the 304th Antiaircraft Battalion are to remain in the front line.

Since the Staff of the 69th Panzer Regiment was transferred to Commander in Chief, West (France), the local tank reserves for immediate counterattacks were reorganized as follows: "Group Cori" : One platoon of the 653d Antitank Battalion (Ferdinands), and one company of the 1st Battalion 4th Panzer Regiment (Panther tanks); "Group East" :
Located between Genzano and Velletri, with one company of the 508th Panzer Battalion (Tiger tanks), and one company of the 653d Antitank Battalion (less one Platoon); "Group West" : Situated at Campoleone (F 875405) with the 508th Panzer Battalion, less one company (Tiger tanks), and 1st Battalion 4th Panzer Regiment (less one company) at Pratica di Mare (F 734410).

On 10 April, the Commanding General Fourteenth Army decided that, at the present time, the complete Army Reserves should not be committed in an attack against the eastern position of the beachhead. Therefore, the planned attack was to be carried out merely as a counterattack after the expected Allied offensive. A strength report by Fourteenth Army dated 10 April, showed a total combat strength of 70,400 men in comparison to 65,800 for the previous month. This included all attached units of the Air Force, SS, SS-Police in Rome, Antiaircraft, Paratroopers, but no rear echelon troops, supply units, or foreign auxiliary (Hilfswillige).

B. Intelligence Report

Documents found on dead enemy soldiers established the location of the 238th Engineer Company of the 1st Engineer Battalion of the 1st Infantry Division (Br), 1.5 km north of Milestone 11 on Highway 82 (F 782300 to F 922289). An artillery observation plane was observed landing 4 km southwest of Borgo Montello (F 976236). Thus the existence of the advanced airfield which was recognized on aerial photographs was confirmed.

The use of 4 cm rapid-fire guns, probably self-propelled, west of Fta Campo di Carne (F 863284) was observed. At several points, the enemy employed phosphorous shells with combination fuse.

C. Statistics

German losses: 82 killed, 403 wounded, and 14 missing.

Allied losses: 11 prisoners.

XLVIII. 14 - 18 APRIL 1944

A. Operations Report

On 15 April, the enemy captured two advanced strong points 6 km southwest of Littoria (G 0818). After a preparatory artillery fire he attacked with two companies, each supported by 6 tanks. German losses were 3 killed and 46 missing in the 735th Infantry Regiment, 16 Italians of Battalion "Barbarigo" were also missing. 3 Allied tanks were destroyed by mines. It is not planned to recapture these strongpoints due to lack of forces in this sector. On 18 April, the enemy repulsed a raid on a strongpoint, 1.75 km northwest of Borgo Piave (G 053203), and pushed forward into our main line of resistance. He was thrown back by a counterattack. Our artillery activity remained unchanged.

During the night of 17 April, both battalions of the 16th SS Panzer Grenadier Division employed on the beachhead front, (2d Battalion 35th SS Regiment, and 2d Battalion 36th SS Regiment were relieved by the 1028th Panzer Grenadier Regiment, and transferred to the area of Florence.

In the sector of the 1028th Regiment, on the right flank of the 362d Infantry Division, the I Parachute Corps took over the area vacated by the battalion furthest on the right. The Corps boundary now runs in a northsouth line through the western edge of Cle Carano (F 940309). To protect the area of Terracina against a landing a strong point is being established at the road junction 8 km northwest of Terracina, and switch positions in the mountains north of Terracina are being prepared.

B. Intelligence Report

According to prisoners of war, the 1st and 2d Battalion 30th Infantry Regiment of the 3d Infantry Division (US) have been withdrawn from the front, and are now in the area north of Anzio. The enemy organized an assault detachment from volunteers of several companies of these units. This assault detachment was ordered to take over a sector temporarily, and to launch raids from it.

On 18 April, during an attack on the Aqua Bianca road, between the Mussolini Canal and Littoria (G 085190), phosphorescent smoke, which adheres to clothing and weapons, was encountered for the first time. The estimated enemy ammunition expenditures, 84,000 rounds. Two ammunition dumps were hit and set on fire.

During the last few days, the enemy tactics changed in the northeastern and eastern part of the beachhead. In the Carano sector (F 940309) artillery shelling increased to heavy barrages. Enemy

reconnaissance patrols were more active. A prisoner of war
stated that the 3rd Infantry Division (US) is in action again.
Whether this is in preparation for an attack or to relieve the 45th
Infantry Division (US), has not been ascertained.

C. Statistics

German losses: 97 killed, 342 wounded, and 82 missing.

Allied losses: 12 prisoners and 4 tanks destroyed.

XLIX. 19 - 23 April 1944

A. Operations Report

In addition to the usual raids along the entire beachhead front,
hard fighting developed for the German strongpoint in the northern
section of the Vallicelli Grandi woods at (F 898294), 4.5 km southeast of Aprilia. After preparatory mortar fire, the enemy temporarily penetrated the strongpoint during the night 21 to 22 April.
During the following night, an enemy attack in battalion strength
was repulsed. On 23 April, the enemy advanced behind a smoke screen
and succeeded in penetrating the southern part of the position.

On the eastern front enemy thrusts were repelled and supporting
tanks turned away by our own artillery fire.

During the night 22 to 23 April, all available artillery of the
Fourteenth Army fired surprise concentrations on enemy positions,
according to plan "Blumenkohl", with good results. Subsequently, it
was ordered to discontinue all scouting for 48 hours to confuse the
enemy as to our intentions. The enemy replied by heavy artillery
fire.

The 3rd Panzer Grenadier Division has requested relief from
front line duty. The division has been employed at the front since
the landing in January and has sustained more than 4,000 casualties.
The Commanding General of the Fourteenth Army suggested replacement
by the 29th Panzer Grenadier Division, as at present no major engagements are expected on the beachhead front.

B. Intelligence Report

According to prisoner of war interrogations, the 13th Brigade
is located in the western coast sector. The 15th Brigade joins the
right flank of the 13th Brigade. The 56th Infantry Division (Br) has
been withdrawn from the front. The bulk of the division is at Naples
for shipment to England. The 5th Infantry Division (Br) has received
the heavy weapons and vehicles of the 56th Infantry Division and has
marked the vehicles with its own insignia.

Prisoners of war of the 2nd Cameronians state that Company B 2d
Cameronians of the 13th Brigade of the 5th Infantry Division was wiped
out and has not been reactivated. Several officers of the battalion
were said to be on leave in England.

6th Gordons 2d Brigade of the 1st Infantry Division (Br) is
located 2 km west of Tre di Padiglione (F 920282) according to
prisoners of war of Company C. The battalion is said to have been
in the front line for one week.

According to a captured officer of the 7th Infantry Regiment
3d Infantry Division, the 45th Infantry Division (US) was relieved

by the 3·d Infantry Division 8 days ago and is in rest north of Anzio.

The 3.d. Battalion 30th Infantry Regiment of the 3·d Infantry Division is located at Cle Carano (F 940309), according to captured documents.

km
Barking dogs north of the Rubbia wood, 1.5/west of Ponte Rotto (F 997314), seemed to indicate employment of watch-dogs.

Estimated enemy ammunition expenditure: 78,000 rounds.

The German High Command, Propaganda Section, rebroadcast the following British report:

"Beachhead at Anzio was 3 months old on the 22 April. During this time, 3,889 enemy soldiers were taken prisoner. The Germans fired an average of 2,000 artillery rounds a day, while the Allies fired many times that amount."

C. Statistics

German losses: 107 killed, 340 wounded, and 48 missing.

Allied losses: 9 prisoners, 3 aircraft downed by small arms, 1 tank destroyed, and 3 trucks destroyed.

During the three months since his landing at Nettuno, the enemy suffered the following losses:

prisoners counted: 6,700 (of which 2,350 are American)
estimated killed : 7,000
estimated wounded: 23,000
tanks and armored scout cars (destroyed) : 249
heavy infantry weapons (captured) : more than 500
airplanes downed: 235
8 warships and 60,000 Register tons of shipping sunk.
39 warships and 376,000 Register tons of shipping damaged.

L. 24 - 28 APRIL 1944

A. Operations Report

The enemy penetrations into the northern part of the Vallicelle Grandi Forest (F 898294) could not be pushed back, during 23 and 24 April, nor could a smaller enemy penetration south of Spaccasassi (F 917330) be prevented. Only on 25 and 26 April, were these two penetrations wiped out. At the Vallicelle Grandi Forest, the 30th Regiment 3d Infantry Division (US) was granted a one hour truce on 25 April to recover their dead and wounded. In the morning of 25 April, after heavy artillery preparations, tank supported enemy attacks were repelled 2 km east of Cle Carano (F 940310). Covered by a smoke screen, the enemy withdrew.

On the 25th, 26th, and 27th, concentrated artillery fire was directed at enemy batteries and supply depots. Extensive fires and effective hits were observed.

Air activity was livelier than ever. In the evening of 28 April, about 20 enemy vessels and 3 motor torpedo boats were observed off the mouth of the Tiber. The 3d Panzer Grenadier Division claimed that the heavy losses, during the last few days, were caused by heavy infantry weapons and not by artillery fire which previously had inflicted 80 percent of all losses.

Commencing on 21 April, Fourteenth Army Command issued various orders: Only defensive measures are considered. The centers of main effort are expected at Aprilia (F 975333) and Cisterna (G 0232). The enemy will lay down a tremendous barrage on our main defense area prior to his major attack. Thereby, he will attempt to break through our front line with a minimum loss of his own troops. For this reason, the defense area is ordered to be enlarged to a depth of 3 to 4 km . It will contain strong points and switch positions, on which artillery fire will be less effective; after a day long heavy barrage fire, some strong points will still be operative. Each artillery battalion will place in reserve one battery which will not fire at present.

Orders were given for the construction of several switch positions between the eastern front of the beachhead and the mountains; e.g. Borgo Isonzo (G 090158) - Sezze, Cisterna (G 0232) - Norma, etc., in order to block the coastal plain against attacks from the south. In case that the beachhead breaks open, the two divisions committed in that area will delay the enemy approach to line C, as long as feasible.

The reinforced 71st Panzer Grenadier Regiment, located about 10 km south of Rome, returned to its division. Thus, the complete 29th Panzer Grenadier Division was assembled northwest of Bracciano Lake, as Army Group Reserve. The 90th Panzer Grenadier Division, less the reinforced 200th Regiment, formerly with the Tenth Army, will be transferred on 26 April, into the area between the mouth of the Tiber and the beachhead, as Army Group Reserve.

Elements of the 26th Panzer Grenadier Division, mainly, the 9th Panzer Grenadier Regiment, will be transferred to the area east of Sezze on 26 April as Army Group Reserve.

B. Intelligence Report

The presence of the Duke of Wellington Regiment 3d Brigade of the 1st Infantry Division (Br), was confirmed 1.5 km northwest of Cantoniera (F 863282) from prisoners of war. This battalion relieved units of the 18th Brigade on 21 April, after it had been brought up to full strength.

The presence of the 1st Battalion 30th Infantry Regiment, of the 3d Infantry Division (US) was confirmed north of Cle Biadaretto, 1 km north of Cle Padiglione (F 921289). The 2d Battalion is on the right, and the 3d Battalion is in reserve according to prisoners of Company C. The Biadaretto Highway (F 919308), towards the northwest, is probably the boundary between the 7th Infantry Regiment and the 30th Infantry Regiment of the 3d Division. The 15th Infantry Regiment is probably employed on the right flank of the 30th Infantry Regiment in the area of Carano. In the last few days, the enemy increased his propaganda with loudspeakers and leaflets inviting our troops to desert.

The enemy fired smoke shells, ejecting smoke pots which screen the entire area over which the shells explode. Shells were observed bursting in the air, leaving 2 smoke trails, and releasing red and green smoke after impact.

Local reliefs took place mostly in battalion strength. It is assumed that two-thirds of the 5th and 1st Infantry Divisions (Br) are committed on the front, and one-third is held as local reserve. Total strength of the American reserves is unchanged. The 3d Infantry Division (US) relieved the 45th Infantry Division (US). It is imperative in order to give a correct estimate of the enemy situation to know the location of the 56th Infantry Division (Br).

Even if this division has not been withdrawn from the beachhead, but is located in the area of Anzio for rest, no major enemy attack can be expected within the next few days.

In a detailed statistical report, the Intelligence Officer made the following calculations: From 29 February to 25 April, the strength of the Fourteenth Army, including the coastal defense units of Tarquinia, and the rear areas were reduced by 42,800 men, by about 170 guns and 125 tanks through transfers and losses. The Allies, however, increased their forces on the beachhead by about 13,000 men, 48 guns, and 104 tanks. The statistics gave the actual strength of German units, the Allied figures were based on the T/O strength of the organization identified.

C. Statistics

German losses: 116 killed, 447 wounded, and 56 missing.

Allied losses: 43 prisoners, 5 tanks destroyed, and 1 airplane downed by small arms fire.

LI. 29 APRIL – 3 MAY 1944

A. Operations Report

Patrol activity continued. At the northern edge of the Michele Gorge (F 835318) and at the Vallicelle Grandi Forest (F 898294), there was stubborn fighting for advanced outposts, which resulted in local successes for our forces. The enemy suffered heavy losses during counterattacks. On 29 April, our advanced strongpoint at (G 035284) 4 km southeast of Cisterna was recaptured with the help of Goliaths. On 1 May, an enemy assault supported by tanks 4 km southwest of Littoria (G 085189) was repelled.

Enemy artillery and naval guns were very active especially during the night. Dummy batteries and other deceptive measures were employed to mislead artillery fire. In the morning of 30 April, enemy ships 20 to 30 km off the mouth of the Tiber were observed. The enemy Air Force was very active.

On 3 May, in the presence of Marshal Kesselring, Fourteenth Army Staff and the Divisional Commanders conducted a war game, which was based on the following estimate of the enemy situation in Italy as of 30 April:

Regrouping of enemy units on the main front is continuing. The sector of the British Eighth Army has been broadened to the south. Three to four infantry divisions and one to two armored divisions have been assembled behind the US Fifth Army. An offensive against the southern flank of the Tenth Army may be launched, simultaneously with an envelopment of the southern flank by a landing at Gaeta. In connection with these operations, there is the possibility of a landing at Terracina and Cap Circeo to connect the two fronts. It is also possible that available Allied Reserves will be used for a landing between the beachhead and the mouth of the Tiber, or farther to the north at Tarquinia, Civitavecchia, or Palo. In each of these cases, attacks from the beachhead, probably with the main effort at Aprilia (F 875333) are anticipated.

B. Intelligence Report

According to prisoners of war, the 13th and 17th Brigades are employed in the area of the 5th Infantry Division (Br). Prisoners of the 2d Inniskillings stated that the 2d Cameronians were on the left of the 2d Wiltshire on the right flank of their unit. These units all belonged to the 13th Brigade. Prisoners from the 2d Northamptons were taken 1 km north of Highway 82 at (F 825295); they stated that the 6th Seaforth and the 2d Royal Scots Fusiliers had joined their unit. All are elements of the 17th Brigade.

It was assumed that in the beginning of April, 1,000 men arrived from England. Of these, 400 landed at Anzio on 15 April. A troop transport convoy from England with 50,000 men is supposed to be on its way to the Mediterranean Theater. Captured documents of the 9th King's Own Yorkshire Light Infantry indicated that elements of the Independent 18th Infantry Brigade were still available for commitment.

Estimated enemy ammunition expenditure: 93,000 rounds.

C. Statistics

German losses: 132 killed, 531 wounded, and 11 missing.

Allied losses: 140 killed, 23 prisoners, 2 tanks destroyed, and 1 airplane downed.

LII. 4 - 8 MAY 1944

A. Operations Report

All infantry battalions of the 92d Infantry Division were committed in strongpoints of the coastal sector Castiglione - Mouth of Tiber. Units of the 29th Panzer Grenadier Division were drawn up closer to the coast to strengthen the defense. Frequent enemy light bomber attacks were reported. Chiefly scouting and raiding occurred in the main sectors of the beachhead. During the night of 6 to 7 May, several enemy attacks, in company strength, were repulsed on the northwestern front of the beachhead.

During the morning of the 8th, an attack, by a company and 10 tanks, near the Rubbia wood (F 984313) was forced to withdraw.

Enemy artillery activity remained static, with occasional surprise barrages. There was considerable increase of artillery fire during raiding operations. Naval artillery fired intermittently on the right flank.

Enemy aerial activity was strong when weather conditions permitted.

B. Intelligence Report

Prisoners of war of the 1st Loyal and 2d Brigade of the 1st Infantry Division (Br) stated that their battalion relieved the 6th Gordons of the same Brigade. This unit is in the area 1 km north of Highway 82 (F 893285).

C. Statistics

German losses: 106 killed, 410 wounded, and 5 missing. Allied losses: 5 prisoners, 2 tanks destroyed, and 2 planes downed.

A. Operations Report

In comparison with the past few weeks, scouting and raiding has decreased. Minor enemy attacks were repulsed. Our raid to blast the bridge .75 km east of Isola Bella (G 006294), failed. Generally, the terrain is considered to be passable for tanks. The enemy airforce has been very active. Complaints have been made about the weakness of our aerial defenses. Heavy air raids were reported from northern and central Italy.

Artillery activity on both sides was the same except for occasional enemy surprise bombardments of shift points. Estimated enemy ammunition expenditure: 89,000 rounds. At 2300 on 11 May, the enemy artillery began concentrated firing preparatory to the offensive on the main front in Italy, which began on 12 May. Simultaneously, the shelling lasted for an hour on the whole beachhead front and increased to heavy barrage fire in the northern sector. The enemy repeated the shelling on the morning of 13 May. At noon, on 12 May, Terracina was shelled by 1 cruiser and 2 destroyers. In the evening of the same day, all troops not committed in the front line were ordered to be ready to move. The impending major attack from the beachhead and landings north and south of the beachhead were expected at any hour. It was ordered that land mines be laid behind the lagoons between the beachhead and Cap Circeo.

The 90th Panzer Grenadier Division, except for one assault gun battalion which is attached to the I Parachute Corps, was marched in the direction of Frosinone in the Tenth Army sector in the evening of 13 May. The GHQ 525th Heavy Antitank Battalion (Hornets) parts of which had been committed at the front of the I Parachute Corps also was marched to the Tenth Army sector. One company of the 1st Battalion 4th Panzer Regiment (Panther tanks) was transferred to the Tank "Group West", to replace these units.

B. Intelligence Report

From captured documents it was established that Company E, 2d Battalion 157th Infantry Regiment of the 45th Infantry Division (US) was at Biadaretto, 1 km north of Torre di Padiglione (F 921289), and that Company C, 133d Infantry Regiment of the 34th Infantry Division (US), was .5 km north of Borgo Podgora (G 045240).

Since 11 May, naval activity in the Anzio-Nettuno harbor has increased. Movements of large freighters and landing craft indicates the arrival of large reinforcements.

C. Statistics

German losses: 77 killed, 357 wounded, and 27 missing. Some who had been reported as missing have deserted. Most deserters are from Italian units.

Allied losses: 4 prisoners, 1 tank destroyed, and 1 spitfire captured in emergency landing.

A. Operations Report

Usual patrol activity, with small forces, took place on both sides. On 17 May, the enemy attacked in battalion strength 4 km south of the east edge of Cisterna (G 0232). The attack was repelled.

Artillery activity consisted of heavy surprise concentrations. Coordinated fire, from 20 to 25 enemy batteries, occurred several times daily, mostly in the early hours of the morning. Our artillery shelled enemy lines and targets in the rear area. Total enemy ammunition expenditure: 125,000 rounds.

Air activity increased over the front with frequent attacks by fighter-bombers in the sector of Sabaudia - Terracina, and heavy air raids on coastal towns north of the Tiber.

During the morning of 15 May, Terracina was shelled from the sea. On 14 May, in connection with the Allied offensive on the main front in Italy, Field Marshal Kesselring issued a proclamation to the soldiers of the Army Group C. This was accompanied by the following order of the day by the Commanding General of the Fourteenth Army:

"Soldiers of the Fourteenth Army!

You who fence in the enemy on his beachhead and you who guard the coast:

On 12 May, the enemy launched his offensive against our comrades of the southern front. This tremendous attack between the coast and Cassino will not be a separate action. At any time, the enemy may also begin an attack against us. We are prepared.

In months of hard work you have dug in well. Enemy barrages will not break our defense line. But do not relax during these barrages.

Our defense is well planned and organized. Our artillery will do its utmost to help the infantry soldiers and the paratroops at the front. Lately, we have used less ammunition, and, therefore, have been able to save enough for the expected major attack.

No tank must penetrate our main line of resistance. Keep your antitank weapons ready and use them when they will be most effective.

There will be no withdrawals either on the beachhead or on the coast. Penetrations might occur, but enemy breakthroughs cannot be tolerated.

Once again, check all preparations, weapons, and supplies. In case reinforcements or materials are needed, request them immediately.

The decisive battle is imminent. We must and we will succeed. I have full confidence in you, my gallant soldiers, because the past five years of war have shown in an amazing way to what extent the German soldier is capable of almost miraculous performances.

Long live the Führer!

von Mackensen."

The piecemeal withdrawal of Fourteenth Army reserves, for the Tenth Army continued even though the Fourteenth Army Chief of Staff repeatedly complained about it to the Army Group.

On 15 May, one company of the 26th Panzer Regiment was transferred to the Tenth Army. On 16 May, the 1st Battalion of the 9th Panzer Grenadier Regiment was transported to Fondi in the Tenth Army sector, via the railroad tunnel north of Terracina. On 17 May, the remainder of the Regiment and the 26th Panzer Reconnaissance Battalion were moved to Pico, 25 km north of Terracina.

On the morning of 18 May, the Commanding General Fourteenth Army called Field Marshal Kesselring by telephone and reported as follows:

"All indications, including enemy orders intercepted on 17 May, lead to the conclusion that the enemy offensive is imminent. While the Tenth Army can withstand enemy attacks by withdrawing step by step without operational danger, the Fourteenth Army must unconditionally hold its present main line of resistance, and must prevent further landings. These landings are to be expected between the main front and the beachhead. A strategic landing north of the Tiber seems improbable at the present moment, unless troops are moved up from North Africa.

A large part of the tactical reserves has been removed from the Fourteenth Army. The Commanding General of the Fourteenth Army requested that at least one reinforced regiment of the 29th Panzer Grenadier Division still stationed as Army Group Reserve north of the Tiber, be attached to him. (Field Marshal Kesselring declined, but he agreed that the 67th Panzer Grenadier Regiment of the 26th Panzer Division should be transferred to the area of Pontinia. There it can be used as local reserve for the east front of the beachhead and will also be available for both the area of Terracina and the right flank of the Tenth Army)."

During the evening of 18 May, the remainder of the 26th Panzer Division, less two battalions of the 93d Artillery Regiment was moved to the Tenth Army. To replace the 67th Panzer Grenadier Regiment, the reinforced 1027th Panzer Grenadier Regiment was transferred from the northwestern front of the beachhead to Pontinia. Staff and two companies of the 1st Battalion 4th Panzer Regiment (Panther tanks) were transferred into the area of Littoria. One company of "Panther" tanks was moved up to Cori and only one remained at Pratica di Mare.

B. Intelligence Report

Prisoners of war state that the 5th Reconnaissance Battalion, 5th Infantry Division (Br) is located north of Highway 82 (at F 809297).

Prisoners of the Royal Electric and Mechanic Engineers 17th Brigade of the 5th Infantry Division (Br) state that their Battalion is employed at the north edge of Anzio. Company F 2d Battalion 179th Infantry Regiment of the 45th Infantry Division (US) is located at Ele Campo dei Pesci.

The 3d Battalion 180th Infantry Regiment of the 45th Infantry Division (US) is now employed northwest of Carano. It is assumed that this Battalion has taken over the sector of the 2d Battalion 30th Infantry Regiment.

A small vehicle which ejected a jet 60 meters wide, probably phosphorous, was observed near Cle Carano (F 940309) approaching the main line of resistance. Two minutes later, the vehicle exploded.

C. Statistics

German losses: 92 killed, 334 wounded, and 5 missing.

Allied losses: 31 prisoners and 2 planes downed by small arms.

LV. 19 - 22 MAY 1944

A. Operations Report

On the beachhead, action continued in the same manner as it had since March.

During the evening of 19 May an enemy attack against the strongpoint at the northern edge of the Vallicelle Grandi forest (F 898294) was repelled. On the 20th the enemy succeeded in penetrating the main line of resistance for a short time 2 km north-northeast of Borgo Podgora (G 045240). The penetration was made under cover of smoke screens in the sector of an Italian unit. Fifteen Italians were shot for cowardice in the face of the enemy. Subsequent attacks at that point on 20 and 21 May were repulsed or wiped out by counterthrusts. On 21 May attacks, partly in battalion strength, between Borgo Podgora and the coast were halted. Every day the enemy artillery repeatedly fired surprise concentrations of 20 minutes in duration.

The enemy Air Force was very active during clear weather, encountering little opposition. Road traffic east of the beachhead had to cease during daylight hours.

While the situation remained unchanged at the beachhead proper, conditions on the left flank of the Fourteenth Army became more and more serious. On 19 May, the German units on the southern flank of the main Italian front were already badly mauled and had been pushed northwest into the mountains. This left the left flank of the Fourteenth Army unprotected, except by the 103d Reconnaissance Battalion stationed around Fondi.

On 20 May, General von Mackensen asked Field Marshal Kesselring during several telephone conversations to assign him the 29th Panzer Granadier Division in order that the rapidly developing gap north of the Terracina-Fondi sector might be closed. The Field Marshal only complied in the evening after air reconnaissance reports had shown that there was no enemy activity in the vicinity of Corsica or Sardinia, which would point to intended enemy landings north of the Tiber. However, at the same time, the boundary between Tenth and Fourteenth Army was moved to the line Sperlonga-Fondi-Vallecorsa-Castro dei Volsci i.e. it now ran in a northerly direction from the coast. This added to the Fourteenth Army zone the southern flank of the main front, which was continuously widening as the enemy advanced in a northwesterly direction. For this reason, the transfer of the 29th Panzer Grenadier Division could not improve the situation at the beachhead front, nor was it made in time to save the situation north of Terracina.

As replacement of the 1027th Panzer Grenadier Regiment (which

had been a reserve unit for the east flank of the beachhead)
the 71st Panzer Grenadier Regiment, with one Artillery Battalion
from the 29th Panzer Division, was moved up during the night of
20 May. Upon its arrival on 21 May it had to be committed north
of Terracina.

B. **Intelligence Report**

The enemy situation remains unchanged.

Estimated Allied ammunition expenditure: 107,000 rounds.

C. **Statistics**

German losses: 62 killed, 234 wounded, and 20 missing.

Allied losses: 10 prisoners, and 1 airplane downed by small
arms.

German artillery losses:

The following guns were lost at the beachhead between
21 April and 21 May. Most of the pieces were destroyed by direct
hits of enemy artillery or bombs, and a few were destroyed by
muzzle bursts: 10 Light guns or light infantry howitzers (7.5 cm),
8 Anti-tank guns 40 (7.5 cm), 6 Anti-tank guns 37 (8.8 cm), 42 Light
field howitzers (10.5 cm), 21 Medium field howitzers (15 cm), 9 Heavy
infantry howitzers (15 cm), 5 Gun 18 (10 cm), 2 Gun 390 (Russian)
(12.2 cm), and 2 Howitzers 18 (21 cm). A total of 107 pieces.

LVI.   23 MAY 1944

A. **Operations Report**

After very extensive artillery preparations, the enemy launched
the offensive, supported by numerous tanks and aircraft, against the
front of the 362nd Infantry Division and on the right flank of the
715th Motorized Infantry Division. Simultaneously he carried out
feints and holding attacks along all other front sectors.

By night, the enemy had succeeded in crossing a section 4 km
wide of the railway line in the center of the 362nd Infantry Division's
sector. His tank units thrust forward to the Cle Fiammingo area, 1 km
east of Cle Lazzaria (F 953365). The attack against the left flank
and the rear of the 3rd Panzer Grenadier Division was sealed off 1.4
km east and 2 km northeast of Spaccasassi (F 917330). In the 715th
Infantry Division's sector, the enemy advanced to the railway bridge
over the Mussolini Canal, 5 km southeast of Cisterna (G 0232). Three
attacks on the 715th Infantry Division's central sector were repulsed,
the enemy suffering heavy casualties.

On the I Parachute Corps sector, the enemy attacked the right
flank of the 4th Parachute Division simultaneously disembarking infantry units in the rear of this division, by local landings. He
thereby succeeded in taking the wooded dunes lying between the former
main line of resistance and l'Americano (F 758315).

At noon, the Commanding General, Fourteenth Army, reported to
the Commander in Chief Southwest, the enemy's breakthrough to the Via

Appia, 5 km southeast of Cisterna (G 0232) and outlined the proposal of the Commander, LXXVI Panzer Corps, which aimed at withdrawing the left flank of the beachhead to the Sezze line. The Commanding General, Fourteenth Army pointed out, that he had no reserves, strong enough to rectify the situation on the LXXVI Panzer Corps' right flank. The proposal was rejected by Field Marshal Kesselring. The situation is to be stabilized by local reserves.

Panzer Division "Hermann Göring" stationed in the Livorno area, left for commitment at the beachhead. Its arrival was expected within two days.

At 1230, Fourteenth Army gave orders that one reinforced Regiment Group of the 92nd Infantry Division, viz. two battalions and one light artillery battalion, commanded by the staff of the 1060th Grenadier Regiment was to relieve the 4th Parachute Division's elements, from their present coastal defense assignment, for commitment with the LXXVI Panzer Corps. In addition, the I Parachute Corps was to withdraw one Regiment Group of the 65th Infantry Division, two battalions with heavy weapons, by the morning of 25 May. This Regiment Group is to be committed as the situation requires.

I Parachute Corps was to move the 29th Panzer Grenadier Division's 129th Motorized Reconnaissance Battalion to the right flank of the LXXVI Panzer Corps.

In the evening, the Commanding General of the Fourteenth Army, ordered that the strongpoint in the Cle Vallicelle Grandi forest (F 898294), be evacuated during the night. In order to shorten the front line, the left flank of the I Parachute Corps was to be withdrawn to a secondary line; Cle Buon Riposo (F 853310) is to be held.

At 2200, I Parachute Corps reported to Fourteenth Army that it believed the enemy was to extend his attack on l'Americano (F 719369). Fourteenth Army assented that the 1st Battalion of the Parachute Assault Regiment should remain in its present sector.

During the night, the Commanding General of the Fourteenth Army, gave the following written order:

"On 24 May, it is of prime importance, to concentrate all forces to prevent an enemy breakthrough.

All heavy antitank guns, assault guns and tanks will be committed at the points where the enemy concentrates his tanks, by ruthlessly depleting all sectors not affected by the attack.

The danger of breakthrough to Velletri necessitates the reinforcement of the severely crippled fighting power of the 362d Infantry Division.

I Parachute Corps will release the following 65th Infantry Division units to the LXXVI Panzer Corps: 65th Fusilier Battalion, 1165th Assault Gun Battalion, and 165th Engineer Battalion (less 1 company). One antitank company of the 92d Infantry Division will also be released to this Corps.

By order of Army Group C, the 94th Infantry Division formerly with the Tenth Army, is subordinated to the 29th Panzer Grenadier Division of the Fourteenth Army effective at 1600 hours. The Division is left with 200 combat men.

B. Intelligence Report

No new enemy units were identified.

The major attack supported by additional Infantry and Armored Units will continue.

C. Statistics

German losses: 15 killed, 35 wounded, and 1 missing.

362d Infantry Division lost 50 per cent of its fighting power. 1028th Panzer Grenadier Regiment of the 715th Motorized Infantry Division lost 40 per cent of its fighting power. 725th Grenadier Regiment of the 715th Motorized Infantry Division lost 40 per cent of its fighting power. 735th Grenadier Regiment of the 715th Motorized Division lost 10 per cent of its fighting power.

Equipment lost: 15 antitank guns 7.5 cm, 12 infantry howitzers 7.5 cm, 30 medium and heavy mortars, and 2 howitzers.

Allied losses: 66 captured, 20 tanks destroyed, and 1 airplane downed.

LVII. 24 MAY 1944

A. Operations Report

In the early morning hours after brief artillery preparations, the enemy continued his attacks on the northern and northeastern fronts of the beachhead. After bitter fighting he was able to cross the Via Appia, 3 km northwest of Cisterna (G 0232) towards the northeast. Several attacks on Cisterna were turned back. In the afternoon and evening, the artillery batteries of the 362d Infantry Division were in close combat with enemy tanks and infantry.

In the sector of the 715th Infantry Division, the enemy penetrated between Cisterna and the Mussolini Canal in the morning. This penetration was stopped at the railroad; in the afternoon, the enemy succeeded in crossing the line.

With permission of the Commander in Chief Southwest, at dusk, the southern flank of the 715th Infantry Division was withdrawn to the Norma Line. The 29th Panzer Grenadier Division in the area north of Terracina, received orders to withdraw; it was to maintain contact with the 715th Infantry Division in the west, and with the Tenth Army in the east. The defense of Monte Calvilli was emphasized, since this point effects the supply line of the Tenth Army.

On the northern front of the beachhead, the penetration of the previous day in the 4th Parachute Division sector was eliminated by counterattacks. The old main line of resistance was reestablished, and heavy losses inflicted on the enemy.

The 3d Panzer Grenadier Division turned back several enemy attacks, especially near the highway Cle Carano (F 940309) - Spaccasassi (F 917330).

With consent of Army Group C, I Parachute Corps, during the night of 24 to 25 May, withdrew its main line of resistance to a secondary line in order to release troops. Preparations are to be made facilitating a further withdrawal to the B-line during the night of 25 to 26 May. Execution of the withdrawal is to take place on Army order only.

Army Group C orders that officers will be assigned to Velletri, Norma, Cori, and Sezze, to be personnally responsible for the defense of these towns. Emergency fortifications are to be erected. Civilian labor will be used. The rear positions will be manned by garrisons made up of rear echelon troops under the leadership of energetic officers.

In the quiet sectors of the front, raids will be executed to tie down enemy forces.

1060th Panzer Grenadier Regiment (92d Infantry Division) was attached to the LXXVI Panzer Corps. Fourteenth Army ordered the 92d Infantry Division to move a battalion, during the night of 25 to 26 May, from coastal defense into the area 8 km south of Rome. Furthermore, the 3d Battalion 192d Artillery Regiment (88 cm antiaircraft) will be moved forward for employment on the beachhead front.

Fourteenth Army orders the I Parachute Corps to transfer the following units to the LXXVI Panzer Corps: Regiment Staff of the Parachute Assault Regiment with one battalion, and the antitank company; 1st Tiger Company; Regiment Staff 145th Grenadier Regiment and 2d Battalion; and the 3d Battalion of the 8th Panzer Grenadier Regiment (less one company).

After the regrouping is completed, Fourteenth Army (excluding the coastal defense sector between Civitavecchia and the mouth of the Tiber) will be organized in the following manner.

Coastal Sector (between western flank of the I Parachute Corps and the mouth of the Tiber):

One battalion of the Parachute Assault Regiment.

Beachhead:

1st Parachute Corps, the bulk of the 4th Parachute Division, 65th Infantry Division (less 145th Grenadier Regiment and one assault gun company, Engineer Battalion, and the 3d Panzer Grenadier Division (less 8th Motorized Grenadier Regiment, two batteries of the 103d Assault Gun Battalion, and the 103d Reconnaissance Battalion).

LXXVI Panzer Corps:

In the sector of the 362d Infantry Division:
The remainder of the 362d Infantry Division, one
assault gun company (Ferdinands), one company of
the 103d Assault Gun Battalion, 65th Fusilier
Battalion, Parachute Assault Regiment (2 battalions),
165th Engineer Battalion (less one company), and the
129th Panzer Reconnaissance Battalion.

In the sector of the 715th Infantry Division:
the remainder of the 715th Infantry Division, one
Tiger company, one company of the 103rd Assault Gun
Battalion, one battalion of the 8th Panzer Grenadier
Regiment, and the 1060th Panzer Grenadier Regiment.

Combat Group "Fries": 29th Panzer Grenadier
Division, the remainder of the 94th Infantry Division, elements of the 103d Reconnaissance Battalion,
one battalion of the 8th Panzer Grenadier Regiment,
and one company of the 93d Panzer Engineer Battalion.

At 2245, the I Parachute Corps reported to the Fourteenth Army,
that the enemy was attacking since 2145, in the sector of the 3d Panzer Grenadier Division, on a 2 km front. This interferes with the
planned withdrawal. The question now arises whether the 3d Battalion
8th Panzer Grenadier Regiment will be available for the LXXVI Panzer
Corps.

B. Intelligence Report

An attack of the 1st Green Howards 15th Brigade of the 5th Infantry Division (Br) north of Moletta gorge (F 8031 - F 8231) was
supported by the Independent 3d Tank Battalion of the County of London
Yeomanry.

According to reports from agents and foreign radio broadcast,
a landing of the 36th Infantry Division (US) is probable.

C. Statistics

German losses (minus LXXVI Panzer Corps and 4th Parachute
Division): 12 killed, 81 wounded, and 8 missing.

German Artillery losses: 1 assault gun 7.5 cm (direct hit
by artillery). The following pieces were spiked: 3 howitzers
10.5 cm, 2 howitzers 15 cm, and 3 howitzers 22 cm (Mörser), (French).

Damaged: 1 gun 10 cm. Slightly damaged by artillery hits:
1 gun 17 cm, 2 field howitzers 10.5 cm, 1 field howitzer 10.5 cm
(Italian), and 1 field howitzer 15 cm.

Allied losses: 49 prisoners, 25 tanks destroyed, 6 tanks
put out of commission, 1 tank captured, and 2 fighter-bombers
downed.

LVIII. 25 MAY 1944

A. Operations Report

After 0530, the enemy continued his attacks with heavy tank,
artillery, and air support. The main effort was in the area northwest, north, and northeast of Cisterna (G 0232). He succeeded, in
spite of heavy resistance on the part of our troops, in advancing
to a line 3 km south of Velletri - 3 km east of Velletri-Giulianello.
In Cisterna, a weak combat team of 80 men led by the commander of
the 954th Grenadier Regiment of the 362d Infantry Division was surrounded and overcome by superior enemy forces.

During the night, the 3d Panzer Grenadier Division repulsed
repeated heavy enemy attacks in the Spaccasassi area (F 917330) in
hand-to-hand fighting.

On the left flank of the I Parachute Corps, beginning south of
Cle Buon Riposo (F 859310), the main line of resistance was withdrawn
to the secondary line. Strong outposts were maintained at the old
line. Fourteenth Army ordered the immediate strengthening of the
tank defenses at the boundary between the 362d Infantry Division and
the 715th Infantry Division. To accomplish this one company of the
103d Assault Gun Battalion and 8 heavy antitank guns of the Antitank
Battalion of the 4th Parachute Division were shifted from the I Parachute Corps to the LXXVI Panzer Corps.

In order to make the Velletri-Giulianello-Cori road usable,
contact was to be made from east to west between the 362d Infantry
Division and the 715th Infantry Division.

Telegraphic order by Field Marshal Kesselring to the Commanding
General, Fourteenth Army read:

"The defensive battle has now reached its decisive
stage. We must inflict such heavy casualties that the enemy's
aggressive power is reduced. This will only be possible if
the main lines of resistance are defended with the utmost
courage and zeal. I therefore prohibit the withdrawal of
divisions or the relinquishment of any key positions without
my express orders."

During the evening, Field Marshal Kesselring informed the
Commanding General Fourteenth Army that the Reconnaissance Battalion
of the Panzer Division "Hermann Göring" is being moved to the breakthrough sector and will remain under Fourteenth Army orders. However,
the bulk of the Division should be held back for possible commitment
with the Tenth Army.

B. Intelligence Report

From intercepted radio messages, it is believed that the 1st
Armored Division (US) is employed in the Littoria-Cisterna-Lazzaria
area.

Estimated enemy artillery ammunition expenditure: 108,000 rounds.

A. Operations Report

The enemy further developed his attacks. Around midday, armored forces succeeded in br eachingthe defensive position south of Velletri by advancing on both sides of the Appian way and from the east. Between the 362 d Infantry Division and the mountain range the enemy pushed forward, as far as Artena.

In the evening 2d Panzer Grenadier Division "Hermann Göring" attacked from a line west of Labico, their objective being a line 2.5 km north of Giulianello.

In 3d Panzer Grenadier Division's sector enemy infantry and armored units attacked in force, along a broad front, at 1100. Except for a few minor penetrations the attack was repulsed after bitter fighting.

Commanding General, LXXVI Panzer Corps, reported to Commanding General, Fourteenth Army, that 715th Infantry Division had lost the greater part of its heavy weapons. Elements of the division were probably at Cori, Norma and Sezze. Moreover, as there was no signal equipment left, the division could not be employed for some time. Army Group C informed Fourteenth Army that Panzer Division "Hermann Göring" would be subordinated to LXXVI Panzer Corps. The Division is to be committed as a unit. In order to master the situation in the area south of Valmontone, Commander in Chief, Southwest, ordered Tenth Army to transfer the following units to LXXVI Panzer Corps, during the night of 26 to 27 May: a regimental group, comprising two battalions, Staff, 5th Projector Brigade, with one regiment, and two heavy antiair craft artillery battalions. Apart from these reinforcements LXXVI Panzer Corps transferred two Grenadier battalions and two artillery battalions from the 29th Panzer Grenadier Division for commitment with the 715th Infantry Division.

In case of overwhelming enemy pressure, the 29th Panzer Grenadier Division was granted permission to withdraw to a line running along the crests from Rocca Massima, 6 km southeast of Cori, to 4 km southwest of Carpineto, to Roccagorga, southwest of Prossedi. The following Fourteenth Army Order was issued.

During the night of 26 to 27 May, the elements of the I Parachute Corps, south of Aprilia between Cle Buon Riposo (F 859310) and the road intersection 2 km northwest of Tre Spaccasassi (F 917330), will fall back to the B-line, which is approximately 2 km behind the main line of resistance.

The elements to the east of this point will take up a flanking position along a line running east of Cle Mandria (F 902365) over Cle Pedica to a point 3 km southeast of Lanuvio, where it joins the C-line. Effective at 2200, the 362d Infantry Division will be subordinated to I Parachute Corps and will fall back to the C-line in its own sector. Its center of defense will be Velletri. The C-line, coming from the southwest, runs 1 km south of Lanuvio - 1 km south of Velletri - Labico.

At the earliest possible hour on 27 May, Panzer Division "Hermann Göring", under the command of the LXXVI Panzer Corps, will attack the enemy forces which have penetrated as far as Artena. They will drive the enemy back to the line: 4 km southeast of Velletri – 2 km south of Giulianello – Rocca Massima.

B. Intelligence Report

The 760th Tank Battalion was established as attached to the 34th Infantry Division (US). The commitment of the 36th Infantry Division (US) was established through prisoners of the 143d Infantry Regiment taken south of Velletri.

C. Statistics

German losses: Artillery losses inflicted by enemy artillery bombardments: All guns (6 Field Howitzers 15 cm) of 671st Artillery Regiment 715th Infantry Division, all guns (6 Field Howitzers 15 cm) 3d Battalion Artillery Demonstration Regiment, 3 field howitzers self-propelled (10.5 cm), 2 field howitzers self-propelled (15 cm), 1 gun (17 cm), 1 Russian gun (15.2 cm), 1 gun (21 cm).

Allied losses: 45 tanks destroyed, 6 planes downed by small arms.

IX. 27 May 1944

A. Operations Report

The enemy continued his attacks in the area south of Valmontone. He also extended the offensive to the sectors of the 65th Infantry and the 3d Panzer Grenadier Divisions. His main blows are on either side of the Aprilia – Anzio Highway, and on Highway 42E (F 877325 to F 917285) and east of Aprilia. After repeated attacks were repulsed by concentrated fire of all our artillery, the enemy succeeded in making several penetrations in the sector of the 3d Panzer Grenadier Division. Our last antitank guns, were destroyed. The weakened troops were forced to withdraw nearly 1.5 km to Spaccasassi Creek.

During the morning, the enemy advanced towards the new main line of resistance of the 362d Infantry Division. Repeated attacks were turned back.

Parts of the Panzer Division "Hermann Göring" counterattacking, from the area west of Valmontone, against a stubbornly fighting enemy reached the railroad line and the highway west of Artena. During the morning, the enemy succeeded in entering Artena by forcing the Panzer Reconnaissance Battalion "Hermann Göring" to withdraw to the north of the town.

Summarized Army orders for further operations follow.

The Army considers the following to be the intentions of the enemy: First, to make a breakthrough in the area between Aprilia and the Albanese Mountains, in a northwesterly direction; second, to make a breakthrough towards Valmontone with the bulk of its forces, in order to surround the southern flank of the Tenth Army, and to cut off their communications to the rear; and third, new landings on both sides of the mouth of the Tiber are within the realm of possibility.

The I Parachute Corps will hold its present position. In the sectors of the 4th Parachute Division, the 65th Infantry Division, and the 3d Panzer Grenadier Division, a gradual withdrawal to the C-line is probable, and must be prepared for. In the sector of the 362d Infantry Division, which is already in the C-line, the position will be held at all costs. The enemy must be brought to a final halt in front of the line. This order pertains to the entire C-line; it has been issued by Hitler.

It is the main mission of the LXXVI Panzer Corps drive the enemy back to the Velletri - Rocca Massima line, which he has penetrated in the direction of Valmontone. This is essential, in order to secure the western flank of the southern tip of the Tenth Army, and to insure once again its supply line over the Via Casilina, until the southern flank of the Tenth Army has reached the C-line. The Tenth Army has orders to transfer the 334th Infantry Division to the Fourteenth Army. The bulk of the 334th Infantry Division will be brought to the Tivoli sector, and elements of it, probably 2 Battalions to the sector 7 km southeast of Valmontone.

The Italian Parachute Regiment "Folgore" will be attached to the I Parachute Corps to fight a rearguard action.

B. Intelligence Report

The First Battalion 6th Armored Infantry Regiment of the 1st Armored Division (US) is west of Artena, according to prisoner of war statements. This Regiment, together with the 13th Armored Infantry Regiment 1st Armored Division (US), advanced from the Cisterna area toward Artena. The first objective was to be the Via Casilina; then the units were to push westward. Elements of the 36th Infantry Division (US) are to follow closely behind. The 1st Armored Regiment of the 1st Armored Division (US), was on the left flank of the 6th Armored Infantry Regiment. The 1st Armored Division (US) had on its left flank the 34th Infantry Division (US), and on its right, the 3d Infantry Division (US).

C. Statistics

German losses: (only the 4th Parachute Division and the 65th Infantry Division) 8 killed, 32 wounded, and 13 missing.

Allied losses: 32 prisoners, 17 tanks destroyed, and 3 tanks put out of commission.

A. Operations Report

The enemy attacks continued in the western and northern sector of the Fourteenth Army with main effort at Stazione di Campoleone (F 877384), and in the areas southeast and southwest of Lanuvio. Strong infantry and tank forces, part of which had been just brought up, were employed in this attack. All enemy attacks against the front of the 65th Infantry Division were repelled, but the enemy succeeded in making a penetration at the boundary between the 65th Infantry Division and the 3rd Panzer Grenadier Division. The penetration was sealed and a front line reestablished.

Minor enemy attacks against the front of the 362d Infantry Division were repelled. The Panzer Division "Hermann Göring", withstood a strong enemy counterattack west of Stazione di Artena, and continued its attack gaining ground towards Lariano, despite stubborn enemy resistance.

The Commander in Chief, Southwest issued this order.

At the expense of other sectors the enemy concentrates all available forces on his left flank. His reserves which we believed to be located in the rear, in Italy, are committed here almost exclusively. The Commander in Chief, Southwest, will hold central Italy and defend Rome under all circumstances. The right flank of the Fourteenth Army will prevent the enemy from breaking through the C-line. All available reserves will be concentrated in the area of Valmontone, in order to stop the advancing enemy and to repel him towards the south. The construction of the Campagna switch position will be continued at all cost, even if the population of Rome has to be employed.

Summarized Army orders for further operations:

In order to provide new reserves, the I Parachute Corps will withdraw its western flank to the general front line: Cle la Fossa (F 765332) - Ardea (F 787350) - C-line east of Cle Piano di Frasso (F 816380). Strong rear guards will remain in the present main line of resistance. The following units will be transferred and attached to the I Parachute Corps: 334th Infantry Division from Tenth Army; 9th Air Force Field Battalion, at present with 715th Infantry Division (Reinforced by remnants of 7th Air Force Field Battalion it is to be committed between the mouth of the Tiber and the main line of resistance); Assault Battalion of the Service School, Southwestern Theater; Fusilier Battalion of the 92d Infantry Division; and the 811th Panzer Engineer Company (Goliath tanks) to be committed as infantry.

The task of the LXXVI Panzer Corps is to continue the attacks on its western flank, in order to contact the eastern flank of the I Parachute Corps. The C-line is to be reached. In case of further withdrawal of the eastern flank of the Corps and the Tenth Army, contact is to be established in the area 4 km southeast of Sgurgola.

In addition to holding the C-line as the final main line of resistance, and to halting the major enemy attack, scouting and patrolling as well as defensive preparations in the area behind the C-line will be executed. The Italian Battalion "Barbarigo" will be attached to the I Parachute Corps for construction of field fortifications.

B. Intelligence Report

According to prisoner of war statements the 2d and 3d Battalion 147th Infantry Regiment of the 36th Infantry Division (US) are committed south of Velletri. General Ryder is said to be Commanding General of the 34th Infantry Division (US).

C. Statistics

German losses: not reported

Allied losses: 7 prisoners

LXII. 29 May 1944

A. Operations Report

The I Parachute Corps withdrew last night according to plan.

The 4th Parachute Division and 65th Infantry Division repelled several attacks, but the enemy succeeded in penetrating the line. This penetration occurred in the area east of the railroad, making a gap 2.5 km wide and 1.5 km deep in the center of the 3d Panzer Grenadier Division's sector.

During the night, Panzer Division "Hermann Göring" attacked and occupied Lariano and the road to the northeast. Enemy counterattacks were repulsed, and an enemy penetration west of Stazione di Artena was wiped out. During the evening, the right flank of the 29th Panzer Grenadier Division attacked in a southwesterly direction to make contact with Panzer Division "Hermann Göring".

At noon, Fourteenth Army informed Army Group C that the position of 65th Infantry Division was serious. For tank defense, the Division had at its disposal only 6 assault guns, 1 Tiger tank and several antitank guns. Field Marshall Kesselring ordered the antiaircraft artillery of the I Parachute Corps (approximately 14 batteries) be employed exclusively against tanks. Minefields were to be laid in the path of enemy tanks by all available engineers. A breakthrough must be avoided.

Army orders for further operations were:

After the unsuccessful attempt to break through at Via Casilina, the enemy transferred his point of main effort to the area between the Albanese mountains and the coast. According to radio intercepts, one armored regiment and elements of an armored infantry regiment of the 1st Armored Division (US) were transferred to that area. The Army expects the continuation of major enemy attacks in the I Parachute Corps sector southwest of the Albanese mountains to force a breakthrough towards Rome. At the same time, continuous attacks in the direction of Valmontone and stronger thrusts against the eastern flank of the LXXVI Parachute Corps can be expected.

The I Parachute Corps will defend the C-line, prevent an enemy breakthrough, and repel penetrations. The withdrawal of the western flank to the C-line is authorized. The following units and artillery are assigned to the Corps: 5 antitank guns of the 92d Infantry Division, one engineer company of the 92d Infantry Division, one engineer company of the 715th Infantry Division, the Panzer Battalion of the 29th Panzer Grenadier Division (less one company which is employed on the northern flank of the 29th Panzer Grenadier Division), and two antiaircraft battalions (to be transferred by the Commanding General of the Central Italian Airforce).

The penetration in the area of LXXVI Panzer Corps must be reduced as quickly as possible, by converging attacks of Panzer Division "Hermann Göring" and attacks by the northern flank of the 29th Panzer Grenadier Division. Army Group C ordered Battle Group " v Zangen", a reinforced Regimental Group of the 356th Infantry Division, presently employed for coastal defense on the Gulf of Genoa, to transfer to the area Grosseto - Orbetello, as Army Group Reserve.

B. Intelligence Report

According to reliable sources the three regiments of the 36th Infantry Division (US) are committed.

C. Statistics

German losses: no information

Allied losses: 65 prisoners, 3 airplanes downed, several damaged.

LXIII. 30 May 1944

A. Operations Report

The enemy continued his attack on a broad front with heavy artillery fire and strong armored forces. His main efforts were in the northern sector, on the eastern flank, and in the sector of the 65th Infantry Division. All attacks were repelled. On the right flank of the 3d Panzer Grenadier Division, the enemy penetration could be considerably reduced by a counterattack.

The night raid of the Panzer Division "Hermann Göring" in the direction of Artena, encountered an enemy attack supported by tanks. The enemy penetration just west of Stazione di Artena was sealed off.

The right flank of the 29th Panzer Grenadier Division attacked during the night, and gained the line running from 2 km east of Artena to 5 km northwest of Segni.

The Fourteenth Army ordered the withdrawal of the "Ost" Battalion of the 362d Infantry Division from the front line, in order to employ this unit in the construction of fortifications.

During the night of 30 to 31 May, the 2d Battalion (less one company) 755th Grenadier Regiment of the 334th Infantry Division was transferred to the LXXVI Panzer Corps in the area south of Palestrina.

B. Intelligence Report

Prisoners of war revealed that the 108th Antiaircraft Battalion of the VI American Corps was employed northwest of Velletri. Two companies of the 1st Reconnaissance Battalion of the 1st Infantry Division (Br) were established near Cle Campoleone (F 870406). The 46th Tank Battalion (GHQ troops) of the 1st Infantry Division (Br) was identified through captured documents. General Walker has been identified as the Commander of the 36th Infantry Division (US).

C. Statistics

German losses: No reports

Allied losses: 106 prisoners, 28 tanks destroyed, and 1 airplane downed.

LXIV. 31 May 1944

A. Operations Report

The enemy continued his efforts to force a breakthrough in the center of the I Parachute Corps by employing strong infantry and armored units, supported by continuous barrage fire. In heavy fighting, the 65th Infantry Division succeeded in preventing the breakthrough along the railroad line Cisterna – Rome, and in holding a thinly-manned front, which blocked the enemy from northwest Cle Campoleone (F 860406) to a point 2 km northeast from Cle Campoleone. During the night, the right flank of the 3d Panzer Grenadier Division was able to regain the old main line of resistance at the Aprilia – Albano Highway, by counterattacking. In the morning hours, a few enemy tanks penetrated along the Aprilia – Albano Highway in the direction of Cecchina. An enemy breakthrough at the boundary line of the 65th Infantry Division and the 3d Panzer Grenadier Division was prevented.

The enemy managed to infiltrate two battalions at the boundary between the I Parachute Corps and the LXXVI Panzer Corps, and to advance on both sides of the mountain ridge, M. Artemisio, up to 3 km northwest of Velletri. An attack was launched by the Panzer Division "Hermann Göring" from Lariano in a southwesterly direction to close the gap between the two Corps.

The 29th Panzer Grenadier Division will be attached to Tenth Army as of midnight 1 June 1944.

The main mission of the Fourteenth Army for 1 June is: First, the repulsion of further enemy attacks; his main point of effort is assumed to be between the Albanese mountains and the coast. Second, the elimination of enemy penetrations between the I Parachute Corps and the LXXVI Panzer Corps at the earliest possible moment. The 334th Infantry Division, less Combat Group "Jänisch" will be assigned to the LXXVI Panzer Corps. It will be commited along and west of the boundary line between the Fourteenth and Tenth Armies. Combat Group "Jänisch" will remain under command of the I Parachute Corps, until further notice.

The 92d Infantry Division has received orders to transfer to the I Parachute Corps, during the night of 31 May to 1 June, the 3d. Battalion 1059th Grenadier Regiment. It is also to prepare the 1st Battalion 1059th Grenadier Regiment, so that it can be attached to the I Parachute Corps in the evening of 1 June. I Parachute Corps will receive an armored combat team consisting of 10 Tiger tanks and 10 remote-controlled demolition vehicles from the 508th Panzer Battalion.

In the evening, an order by Field Marshal Kesselring emphasized the urgency of eliminating the enemy infiltration between the I Parachute Corps and LXXVI Panzer Corps. This was to be accomplished even though it might be necessary to use all the tanks of the Panzer Division "Hermann Göring", and to withdraw units from the northern flank of the 29th Panzer Grenadier Division.

Available tanks and assault guns on 31 May 1944:

Unit	Tanks	Assault Guns
Parachute Assault Gun Battalion, XI Air Force Corps	3	22 (Italian)
65th Infantry Division		1 (Italian)
3d Panzer Grenadier Division		15
Panzer Division "Hermann Göring"	20	7
508th Panzer Battalion	10 (Tiger)	
1st Company of the 653d Antitank Battalion		2 (Ferdinand)
Total	33 tanks	47 assault guns

B. Intelligence Report

The Fourteenth Army was now facing the following enemy division:

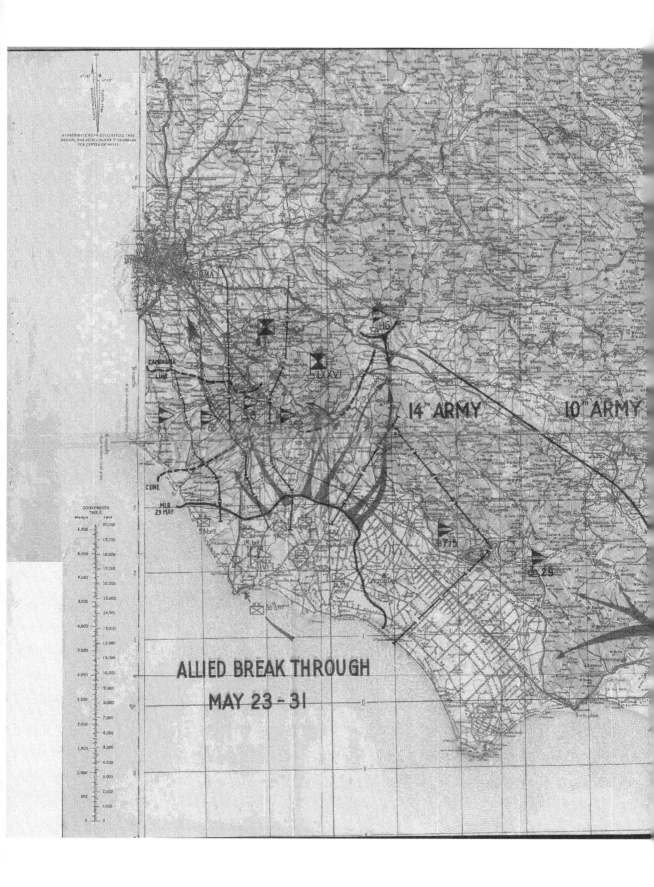

14ᵗʰ ARMY   10ᵗʰ ARMY

LXXVI

CAMPANIA
LINE

C LINE

MLR
23 MAY

ALLIED BREAK THROUGH

MAY 23 - 31

```
         5th Infantry Division (Br)
         1st Infantry Division (Br)
         1st Armored Division (US)
        34th Infantry Division (US)
        36th Infantry Division (US)
        85th Infantry Division (US)
         3d Infantry Division (US)
         1st Special Service Force (US)
        88th Infantry Division (US)
         4th Moroccan Mountain Division (US)
```

Final estimate of enemy situation:

On 23 May, the enemy began his major attack, from the beachhead, with a strong concentration of men and materiel. The objective was to occupy the important heights near Velletri, and then to thrust forward to Valmontòne. This would clear the way for a breakthrough to Rome. His immediate objective was to cut the important Tenth Army supply route to the Via Casilina (Highway 6).

All available forces were concentrated in a spearhead, viz the 1st Armored (US), 3.d. and 34th Infantry Divisions (US), which succeeded in making a deep penetration east of Velletri. Making use of this success, the 36th Infantry Division (US) was brought up and immediately commited at the point of main effort. The attacking force was further strengthened by the 760th Tank Battalion and 178th Artillery Regiment (US). The 1st Infantry Division (Br) was reinforced by the 3d Tank Battalion, County of London Yeomanry.

The enemy changed his tactics from a slow advance to a quick thrust. He attempted to achieve a strategical success by driving a strong tank wedge forward. The battle reached the climax when enemy units from the main front and from the beachhead made contact. The enemy now had a flanking position from which he could attempt to roll up the front of the Tenth Army. At the same time, the possibility existed that he would capture Rome by attacking along the western slope of the Albanese Mountains. Judging from the ships available and the large reserves in North Africa, landings in central and north Italy appeared possible.

C. Statistics

German losses: not reported. Guns destroyed: 1 field howitzer (15 cm) (by artillery fire), 4 assault guns (by artillery fire).

Allied losses: 69 prisoners, 38 tanks put out of commission, 2 airplanes downed; captured: 4 American command and scout cars, 1 armored personnel carrier with equipment, miscellaneous equipment.

Prior to the landings, the first phase of the Anzio operation appeared pre-determined for the defender, by depleting the coastal area of Rome, while the first days after the landings were decisive for the Allies. All engagements thereafter, were the result of the above fact.

After the Allies had successfully invaded southern Italy, the main task of the German High Command was to prevent Allied advances by defending on a stabilized defensive front, since the German forces were not numerous enough to eliminate the Allies from the Italian mainland. This was accomplished, until the beginning of 1944, by means of the Gaeta – Ortona line (Bernhard or Gustav Position).

As continued attacks against this line promised little success for the Allies, the German High Command believed that Allied tactics would have to change and amphibious moves be planned. It was believed that these landings were intended to cut the supply lines of the German Tenth Army and neutralize the Bernhard position. Due to the small number of German troops in Italy, successful enemy landings, supported by intensified Allied attacks against the southern front, could have created a critical situation. The Allies had apparently recognized this and prepared for a landing, by attacks at the Garigliano River. It was believed that the immediate Allied intentions were to break through at the Garigliano, but to pin down German frontline units and draw German reserves forward. A break-through of the Bernhard position was only to be expected in conjunction with a successful amphibious operation against the weakened German rear areas.

This danger was recognized by the German High Command. Therefore, at the beginning of the Allied offensive on 18 January, Army Group C intended to reinforce the Garigliano front, without weakening the coastal defenses of central and upper Italy. Allied tactics simplified the task of Army Group. When only the US Fifth Army attacked in the sector south of Cassino on 18 January, the Germans were able to withdraw and transfer troops from the sector of the British Eighth Army, to reinforce the Cassino sector. The German High Command made the error of not transferring a maximum of forces at the outset of the offensive, but delayed until the situation became grave and the Allies threatened with a break-through on the Garigliano. To prevent this, all readily available German forces in the area of Rome and its coastal sector had to be committed.

As a result, the Allied success in the offensive south of Cassino was not only established, but increased in scope. Army Group C was compelled to commit all its troops along the defense line, including the reserves. It was also forced to relieve its units from the coast defenses west of Rome as reinforcements for the south. This created the favorable vacuum for successful Allied landings at Anzio.

The VI Army Corps (US) encountered no organized resistance, during the landings on 22 January, as there had been no leakage of the plans for the intended landing and, consequently, the German coastal defense forces were not alerted. The Allies landed during the night of the 21 to 22 January, and formed several small bridgeheads which were consolidated and expanded during the 22 January. The following two days, the beachhead forces did not attack, but concentrated on landing further reinforcements and securing the beachhead.

Due to this stand-still by the invading forces, the supply
lines of Tenth Army remained open, and neither the highways
leading south from Rome nor the Albanese Mountains were denied
to the Germans. It appeared to the German Command that Allied
plans did not contain a precise time-table for an assault against
these objectives, but made this attack dependent on the strength
of the German defending forces.

During the first two days after the landing, the Allies
appeared to make a critical error, in that they did not exploit
the weakness of the German defense by immediately extending the
beachhead on a strategic plane, even though this may have been
contrary to the original plans. The German Command realized that
the loss of the Albanese Mountains or the City of Rome would
have led to an Allied break-through on the southern front.

The fact that the Allies did not immediately exploit this
favorable situation on the beachhead determined the German course
for the entire operation and made it possible for Army Group C to
build a stabilized defensive line on the beachhead until 24 January. Later German reinforcements could be brought up as the
attacks of the US Fifth Army south of Cassino diminished. This
allowed for a release of reserves in this area to the Anzio
sector.

After conclusion of the first phase of the landings, the
German Command considered that neither the attacking Allied
forces nor the defending German forces obtained complete success.
The Allies did not reach their strategic objectives, and the
Germans did not succeed in preventing the landings or in eliminating the Allied Forces before they had established their
positions. By 25 January, both sides had built a stabilized
front line. Thus the beachhead became practically an extension
of the southern front. The battles of the following weeks and
months were fought in accordance with the original objectives
on both sides: the Allies to make a break-through from the
beachhead in a northernly and northeasternly direction, and the
Germans to eliminate the beachhead.

German operations depended on the condition of the terrain
and on the weather. For these reasons, German counterattacks
could only be made in the Aprilia sector, or from the area of
Cisterna, during a period of bad weather when the Allied airforce
and Naval artillery were less effective.

The opportunities for success, during this time, seemed
quite feasible, since the Allied forces on the beachhead appeared
not too strong. The German High Command did plan an attack for
28 January, from the area of Aprilia, to split the beachhead.
However, the concentration of German troops was delayed, because
reinforcements for the attack from upper Italy, France, and
Germany did not arrive in time, due to demolished railroads and
highways. The German High Command then had to postpone the attack
until 1 February. This plan was upset by the Allied attack on
30 January, which began in the area of Aprilia and resulted in a
deep penetration into the German defensive front. The German
High Command was forced to eliminate this penetration and gain
positions for a new counterattack. The penetration was eliminated by 9 February. During the following days, the Germans
prepared a new large-scale attack which, depending on weather
conditions, was scheduled for 15 February.

The attack, favored by good weather, began on 16 February.
On 17 February, Highway 82 across the beachhead was traversed
between Fta Campodi Carne and Cle Tre di Padigliones. It was the

opinion of the German High Command that the development of this attack would create a crisis on the Allied side, this, if properly exploited, could lead to a complete German success. Fourteenth Army, however uncertain, whether sufficiently deep penetrations in the Allied line had been made, by the evening of the second day of the attack, did not commit its available reserves at that time. In addition, the terrain was not suitable for tank employment as had been presumed. Fourteenth Army, having no faith in the possible success of a break-through without supporting tanks, held back its reserves. This decision brought the attack to a standstill on 18 February, and the final success appeared to be in no proportion to the strength committed.

As a result of these experiences, Army Group C abandoned the original plan of eliminating the Allied beachhead by an all-out, large-scale attack. The revised intentions were to reduce the beachhead by limited attacks against smaller objectives. The German artillery, concentrated around the beachhead, was to interfere with Allied concentrations, which might be preparing for a major attack. With these tactics, the German High Command hoped that the Allies would evacuate the beachhead as soon as they realized a further strategic extension could not be executed.

The first German offensive, under these plans, was made on 29 February, from the area of Cisterna with the Astura as the primary objective. A secondary and more strategic action was envisaged if the attack were successful. However, unfavorable terrain for tanks due to weather, halted the assault. Later German counterattacks of this type were of smaller scope, because of the strong local reactions of the Allies, and the situation on the Tenth Army front rarely permitted the concentration of strong German assault forces in the Anzio sector.

As a result the Allies, in the months that followed, were unable to enlarge the beachhead to any extent, while Fourteenth Army was not able to eliminate it. Only in the latter part of May, were the Allies able to break through the German defensive front on the beachhead, and reach their original objectives. The German High Command did not believe that this success resulted from engagements on the beachhead, but rather from the effects of the successful Allied offensive against the southern flank of Tenth Army, causing a collapse of the German defensive front south of Cassino.

ANNEX I

Order of Battle of German Divisions

Divisions	Type	Infantry* Regiments	Artillery Regiments	Füsilier or Rcn Battalions	(Panzer) Tank units	Antitank Battalions	Engineer Battalions	Antiaircraft units
1	Parachute	1, 3, 4	1	-	-	1	1	1
3	Pz. Gren.	8, 29	3	103 Rcn	103 Bn	3	3	-
4	Parachute	10, 11, 12	4	-	-	4	4	4
5	Mountain	85, 100	95	85 Rcn	-	95	95	-
8	Mountain	296, 297	1057	-	-		1057	-
15	Pz. Gren.	104, 115	33	115 Rcn	115 Rcn	33	33	315
16	SS-Pz. Gren.	35, 36	16	16 Rcn	16 Bn	15	16	16
26	Panzer	9, 67	93	26 Rcn	26 Regt	51	93	304
29	Pz. Gren.	15, 71	29	129 Rcn	129 Bn	29	29	313
44	Infantry	131, 132, 134	96	44 Füs	-	46	80	-
65	Infantry	145, 146, 147	165	65 Füs	1165 Bn**	165	165	-
71	Infantry	191, 194, 211	171	71 Füs	-	171	171	171
90	Pz. Gren.	200, 361	190	190 Rcn	190 Bn**	90	190	293
92	Infantry	1059, 1060	192	92 Füs	-	192	192	-
94	Infantry	267, 274, 276	194	94 Füs	-	194	194	-
114	Jäger	721, 741	661	114 Füs	-	114	114	-
162***	Infantry	303, 314, 329	236	236 Füs	-	236	236	-
278	Infantry	992, 993, 994	278	278 Füs	-	278	278	-
305	Infantry	576, 577, 578	305	305 Füs	-	305	305	-
334	Infantry	754, 755, 756	334	334 Füs	-	334	334	-
356	Infantry	869, 870, 871	356	356 Füs	-	356	356	-
362	Infantry	954, 955, 956	362	362 Füs	-	362	362	-
715	Infantry	725, 735, 1028	671	715 Füs	-	715	715	-
"Hermann Göring"	Panzer	1, 2, "Hermann Göring"	1 "Hermann Göring"	1 Rcn	"Hermann Göring" Regt	1 "Hermann Göring"	1 "Hermann Göring"	-

The role that these divisions played during the Anzio campaign is defined in the preceding text. Since German Corps and Army units were constantly shifted in the course of the campaign, they are not included in this order of battle. The frequent regroupings are described in detail in the text.

* Under infantry regiments are included the parachute regiments of the parachute divisions, and the Panzer Grenadier regiments of the Panzer and Panzer Grenadier divisions.

** In these divisions the tank battalion has been replaced by an assault gun battalion.

*** This unit is composed mainly of "volunteers" from Soviet Central Asia. Its full designation is 162d Infantry Division (Turk).

Order of Battle of British Divisions

Inf Div	Inf Regt	Arty Regt	Engr Bn.	AT Bn	Rcn Bn	AA Bn
1st	24 Gds, 2, 3	2, 19, 67	1	8	1	90
5th	13, 15, 17	9, 91, 156		53		
56th	167, 168, 169	64, 65, 113		67		100

British Units attached to Fifth Army:

    24th, 78th, and 80th Artillery Regiments.
    46th Royal Scots Greys (Armored Battalion)
    6th Queen's Own Hussars (Armored Battalion)
    6th Cheshire (Infantry Battalion)
    2/VII Middlesex (Infantry Battalion)
    1st Rifle Brigade
    40th Marine Commando

Div	Regt.	Arty Bn	Engr Bn	AT Bn	Rcn Bn
1st Armored	1, 13 (armd) 6	27, 68	16	701	81
3d Inf	7, 15, 30	10,39,41,9	10	403	
34th Inf	133,135,168				
36th Inf					
45th Inf	157,179,180	159,160,171, 189		645	
82d Airborne	325,326,504, 505, 509 (Parachute)				

US Units attached to Fifth Army:

    1st Special Service Force Brigade
    1st, 3d, and 4th Ranger Battalions
    36th Engineer Regiment
    191st Armored Battalion
    601st and 894th Antitank Battalion
    751st Tank Battalion

German tactical symbols

A. Unit symbols.

Army Group Headquarters

Army Headquarters

Corps Headquarters

Division Headquarters

Regimental Headquarters

Battalion

Company (infantry)

Company (Panzer)

Mountain (battalion)

Panzer or Armored (battalion)

Antitank (battalion)

Tank Destroyer (battalion)

Antiaircraft artillery (battalion)

Assault Gun (battalion)

Panzer Grenadier or armored infantry (division)

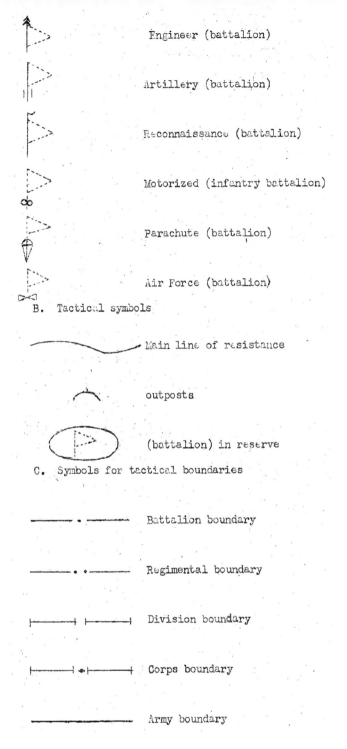

Engineer (battalion)

Artillery (battalion)

Reconnaissance (battalion)

Motorized (infantry battalion)

Parachute (battalion)

Air Force (battalion)

B. Tactical symbols

Main line of resistance

outposts

(battalion) in reserve

C. Symbols for tactical boundaries

Battalion boundary

Regimental boundary

Division boundary

Corps boundary

Army boundary

Description of German units

The following German units do not have corresponding Allied units. Therefore, the designation of these units has been left untranslated in the preceding text.

Jäger division: This type of division was originally designed for mountain and mobile warfare. It is equipped as a light infantry division, consisting of only two infantry regiments.

Panzer division: Consists of a Panzer (tank) regiment, two Panzer Grenadier regiments, a Panzer artillery regiment, a Panzer reconnaissance battalion, an antitank battalion which may be redesignated assault gun battalion, a Panzer engineer battalion, a Panzer signal battalion, an antiaircraft battalion, and services.

Panzer Grenadier division: Consists of two motorized infantry regiments to two battalions each, a motorized artillery regiment, a Panzer reconnaissance battalion, an engineer battalion, an antitank battalion, an antiaircraft battalion, a signal battalion, a tank battalion which is sometimes replaced by an assault gun battalion, and services.

Panzer Grenadier regiment: Consists of two battalions equipped with armored troop carriers, and two regimental support companies; the infantry howitzer company and the engineer company.

Fusilier battalion: Full designation: (Divisions-Füsilierbataillon). It performs both reconnaissance and infantry support functions in infantry divisions. Organization identical with that of infantry battalions, except that it has more mobility bicycles).

Description of German Armor

Type	Gun Armament	Weight short tons	Crew Men	Chassis	Remarks
Pz.III	5 cm	24.6	5		
Pz.IV	7.5 cm	26	5		
Pz.V "Panther"	7.5 cm	50	5		
Pz.VI "Tiger"	8.8 cm	62.75	5		
"Ferdinand" (later "Elephant")	8.8 cm	73	6	Tiger	tank destroyer
Assault Gun	7.5 cm	25.35	4	Pz.III	antitank as well as antipersonnel
Assault Howitzer	10.5 cm	25.8	4	Pz.III	antipersonnel
Assault Howitzer	15 cm	30.4	5	Pz.IV	"
"Hornet" (later "Rhinozeros")	8.8 cm	27	5	Pz.IV	tank destroyer

Remote Controlled Demolition Vehicles:

"Goliath" - line controlled demolition charge (length of wire 2000 yards); explosive charge 200 pounds, total weight 800 pounds; vehicle blows up when its demolition charge is set off.

"B IV" - radio controlled demolition vehicle; explosive charge 800 pounds; total weight 4.5 tons;
The B IV is driven under its own power to the line of departure near the target, usually an emplacement or pillbox. The control transmitter of the radio equipment, retained by the driver when he dismounts, is used to steer the vehicle to its destination. In contrast to the Goliath the B IV is not expendable, but deposits its load of explosive at the target and returns.

Lightning Source UK Ltd.
Milton Keynes UK
UKHW031822190821
389122UK00008B/1461